W9-DAE-384

Suspense in the Formula Story

Suspense in
the Formula Story

George N. Dove

Bowling Green State University Popular Press
Bowling Green, Ohio 43403

Library of Congress Catalogue Card No.: 89-061585

ISBN: 0-87972-455-2 Clothbound
      0-87972-456-0 Paperback

Cover design by Laura Darnell Dumm

Contents

Chapter 1
The Criticism of Formula Fiction

One of the best things that can happen to a novel is for it to gain the reputation of A Book You Just Can't Put Down. This is the book we sit up reading until two a.m., despite the necessity of being up again at seven, or read on the plane and train and at dinner. Such books are Peter Benchley's *Jaws*, Michael Crichton's *The Andromeda Strain*, and Frederick Forsyth's *The Day of the Jackal*, and almost anything by Robert Ludlum or Agatha Christie. The persistence of effect of such books is remarkable, because we are driven not only to continue reading this one but also to watch for the next one by the same author. Such books become treasures to authors and publishers, because they achieve a major purpose of popular fiction: they make money.

Of course a book may have any one of several features that make it hard to put down (style, ideology, informational content, humor), but the one most commonly responsible for the holding-power of a story like *Jaws* is the quality of suspense, the drive that keeps us turning pages. The etymology of "suspense" suggests the nature of this holding power: we are "dangled beneath" or "hung between" until we are brought to a point of stability.

Throughout this discussion, we will be using the term "suspense" in a sense somewhat different from the one to which most book-lovers are accustomed. "Suspense" is commonly used to designate a genre of popular fiction, parallel with Mystery and Adventure. Characteristically, a book-dealer's catalogue will list categories like "English detective," "Hard-boiled American," "Suspense," "Thriller," and the like. As people in the book trade use "suspense" it implies a kind of story characterized by menace, conflict, and violence. When a distinction is needed between the "Suspense Novel" and the "Thriller," "Suspense" refers by custom to the story of the one-versus-one, innocence-in-jeopardy type, like *The Exorcist,* while the

1

"Thriller" is used for the Giant Conspiracy Against Civilization, like *The Holcroft Covenant.*

In this book, we will be using the term in a functional sense, to designate a process, something that happens between a reader and the book he is reading. This is an idea to be developed more fully in Chapter 2. For the present, it will be profitable to consider the definition by David Daiches: "Suspense may be defined as an intensification of interest in what happens next, and is necessary in some degree for all drama and most fiction."[1] Two elements here should catch our attention. First, the essential in the process is the *reader,* because it is only in him that any "intensification of interest" can develop. Second, we are discussing a process that cuts across the lines of several of the traditional genres, "serious" as well as "popular".

Our concern in this book, though, goes beyond the matter of definition. How does one criticize (i.e., interpret) a popular story that relies heavily upon the suspense process? One quick answer is to dismiss it as popular and therefore trivial, or label it a potboiler, lacking depth and hence inappropriate to real criticism. The popular culture critic, however, will insist that the story must be interpreted because it *is* popular, as an index of the contemporary cultural climate; after all Great Ideas can be found in many places, and the scarcity or absence of such ideas in the consciousness of a given era is to the popular culturist a matter of supreme interest. The Mike Hammer novels of Mickey Spillane, enormous best sellers in the 1940s and 50s, offer some highly reliable clues to the state of the public mind of the United States during the McCarthy Era. As D.F. Rauber argues in a particularly insightful essay, popular fictions may be essential documents for the study of intellectual history, for the very reason of the method of their production: "The popular writer—suffering from no delusions of grandeur, pressed for time, and usually working within a formula—has neither the desire nor the opportunity to impose upon his work strongly individualistic elements."[2] He writes, that is to say, what his readers want to read. The critic who needs to know what was going on in the public mind at a given point must study those works that the public found most acceptable.

Such books can not be adequately interpreted without the use of the reader as criterion. Much potentially sound criticism of popular fiction has been ruined by those who habitually go direct to the text of the story, with maybe a side-glance at the author but no consideration of the kind of reader for whom the writer designed that story.

We will lay it down as requisite, then, that the critic seeking to interpret a popular story will hold some kind of conception of the typical/average/representative reader the author had in mind as he wrote it. What the critic learns to do, actually, is to *postulate* a reader, and the success of his interpretation is, in part at least, dependent on the validity of that postulation. More to the point, what the critic projects is the author's image of his reader. Now, whether any given reader—or all of them—fits that image is really irrelevant. What the critic wants is a perception of that process by which the author achieves his artistic purpose with that reader, "real" or projected.

Where, then, do we look for our author's image of this projected reader? We seek it in the text of the story itself, and when we do so, we are reaching for the essence of interpretation in popular fiction. One writer in whom this recognition is relatively easy is Ed McBain, because one reason for McBain's continuing popularity is his closeness to his readers, whom he seems never to forget during the course of composition. One of his favorite devices in the 87th Precinct novels is the in-joke or running gag, which a first-time reader may miss but which delights the 87th Precinct fan. We can recognize McBain's projection of this faithful reader in a little exchange in *Hail, Hail, the Gang's All Here!* where detective Meyer Meyer, one of the series regulars, investigates some disturbances in a residence. The woman who called him makes a casual reference to his age as being around forty or forty-five. "I'm thirty seven." Meyer replies (31).* Now, the joke is that Meyer has been thirty-seven for a dozen or so years, and the woman is actually about right in her estimate. The veteran will catch the point; the newcomer will not. The reader projected by McBain is sympathetic to Meyer, has a sense of humor and a good memory, and has read at least some of the other novels in the series. In Chapter 10 of this book we will see a conveniently matched pair of such projections: the postulated reader of Ian Fleming's *You Only Live Twice* wants a clear, effortless view of the game and likes to be teased, put off, and promised; the reader of John le Carré's *The Spy Who Came In From the Cold* is likely to be sophisticated in the spy formula

---

*A list of editions of novels cited will be found in the Appendix.

and does not object to coping with such subtleties as the ambiguity of appearance and reality. To watch the authors work on these projected images is to perceive the operation of the process of creativity. Now the fact that these two projections may be the same person in actual practice does not change anything as far as our study of process is concerned; here we are interested in that reader the author sees as he writes, because he is the element that shapes the text.

Keeping in mind the supremacy of the reader—the author's projection—we are ready to state a definition of suspense as the term will be used in this book. We will begin with three basic statements that can serve as guides to the viewpoint to be developed in the following pages:

1. Suspense takes place only when the reader is involved in the story.

2. Suspense is dependent to a far greater extent upon thrust than upon delay.

3. The will to read on—that is, intensification of interest in what happens next, or *suspense*—is dependent to a greater degree upon what the reader has been told than upon what he wants to find out. The more the reader knows (without knowing everything), the more he wants to know.

The involvement of a reader naturally takes many forms, but whatever the nature of the participation it is sure to be an expression of some kind of *caring*. Marie Rodell defines suspense as "the art of making the reader care what happens next," a statement that begins where it should, with the reader's reaction.[3] Reading Bram Stoker's *Dracula* we may not actually mutter aloud "Here he is now!" when the Count begins to emerge into one of his dreadful appearances, but the reaction will take place at least on a sub-verbal level, as an expression of the tension building in us and hence keeping us in a state of suspense. Phyllis Whitney describes the activity in terms of the aims of a successful writer: "We want readers to ask, 'What is happening here? What will happen next? Where are we heading?' "[4] The point here of course is that a writer may invent a story built around the most vexing of paradoxes or the most menacing of dangers and still lose his readers if he does not succeed in making them care what happens next.

Some critics apparently take the view that the key to effective suspense lies in the number of obstacles a writer can place in the way of successful resolution, that is, in using the strategy of delay. Thus Roland Barthes lists several "dilatory morphemes" [5] and Dennis Porter says that the "experience of suspension" occurs "whenever a perceived sequence is begun but remains unfinished."[6] We are, moreover, often told that it is the complexity of the puzzle, the apparent impossibility of solution that drives us to finish a good detective story. As we will see in the discussion of *The Greene Murder Case* in Chapter 5, however, it is not the celebrated classic mystery that impels us, or the delays and obstacles placed before us, but the insistent, almost strident voice of the author in the role of Lecturer-Beside-the-Screen that drives us toward resolution. What the writer does is to send us messages and to give us almost surreptitious signals that keep us in the state of tension that creates successful suspense.

Finally, it is not so much what the reader wants to find out as what he already knows that generates the process of suspense. One thing that keeps us interested in a story is our access to privileged information, whereby we know something that has been withheld from the characters themselves and hence enjoy a sense of superiority. The principle is used in a TV quiz show, where the answers are put on video for the benefit of the audience: we are held much more firmly by the knowledge of the answer than any desire to participate in or to compete with the efforts of the contestants. The same principle applies in the reading of a mystery; where we begin to perceive the development of a line of inquiry on the basis of our knowledge of the great detective protagonist, or where we have been gratuitously admitted to some important insight, we are involved in the story. The idea is naturally related to the principle of caring: what we don't know about, we don't care about.

With these principles in mind, we are ready to turn back to our earlier question, How does a critic go about interpreting a fiction designed for popular consumption? In the criticism of the mystery story, at least, there has never been any lack of approaches. Just about every imaginable school of criticism has been used on the mystery: historical, biographical, Freudian, Marxist, feminist, and others. Some of these have been outstandingly successful. Most students of the mystery would class W.H. Auden's study of basic myth, "The Guilty Vicarage," as indispensable to the field. Others have shown a remarkable permanence, like Geraldine Pederson-Krag's "Detective Stories and the Primal Scene," a Freudian interpretation; Francis M. Nevins' biographical study of Ellery Queen *(Royal Bloodline)*, and Dorothy Sayers' Introduction to *The Omnibus of Crime* (historical).

The critic who has come closest to interpretation of the popular story *as* popular story, however, is John Cawelti, who laid down the principles of formula criticism in an essay, "The Concept of Formula in the Study of Popular Literature" (1973) and the book *Adventure, Mystery, and Romance* (1976). Cawelti frames his interpretation of such popular fictions as the detective mystery, the spy story, and the western in terms of the qualities that characterize their type. All of them tend to follow a pattern or formula, which he defines as "a combination or synthesis of a number of specific cultural conventions with a more universal story form or archetype." Literary formulas are thus products and representatives of the culture in which they develop.[7]

Cawelti addresses two aspects of the formula story that have special relevance for the concept of process we are seeking to develop here. The first is that those accepted conventions of formula fiction, those proved, almost endlessly durable devices so familiar to the experienced reader, serve to establish a common ground between writer and reader, so that communication between them is facilitated (8-9). The other is that the formula story promotes a sense of security in the reader by assuring him that, no matter how exciting and disrupting the story, "things will always work out as we want them to."(16) We might amend this second idea by saying that in formula fiction things at least always work out; we may not be happy with the resolution, but we are always assured that there will be one. In the formula story, there is no such thing as an unresolved mystery or a conflict without an ending.

The concept of formula is so naturally related to the idea of process that we need to expand this approach a little further. In Chapter 2 we will be using two terms, formulaic conditioning and formulaic axiom, to designate a part of the "readiness" of a person who reads a suspenseful story. The point is simply that we become conditioned, by our reading experience, to expect certain things in a formula story that we would not ordinarily expect in any other type of reading. For example: One of those signals writers use to stimulate suspense reactions is what we will call the Solitary Figure, which is basically some kind of anomaly—a person, an object, or a relationship— introduced into a story without preparation or explanation. Now, in a non-formula story, solitary figures wander on and off stage for a variety of reasons, serving literary purposes that may be metaphoric, symbolic, or merely atmospheric. Not so in the formula story, especially the mystery: just let a stranger enter the scene and the reader experienced in the mystery formula knows to watch this one especially closely, because a Solitary Figure never shows up in a mystery without some useful reason.

Many critical studies with a Freudian, Marxist, Existentialist, or any of these other orientations, are peripheral interpretations, in that they do not address the formula story as formula story, and hence do not face the basic problems of interpretation. Stories that follow a formula—mystery, spy, supernatural, thriller—are different in purpose from mimetic fiction, and failure to recognize their special qualities may cause a critic to fail in the task of interpretation. Such was the case of Edmund Wilson, whose critical approach to the mystery constitutes a case study in how not to criticize popular formula fiction.

Wilson won the enthusiastic hatred of mystery fans in three pieces he did for his literary column in *The New Yorker* in 1944 and 1945,[8] especially the notorious "Who Cares Who Killed Roger Ackroyd?" the very title of which alone was enough to alienate the dedicated Christie fan. In this one and in "Why People Read Detective Stories" Wilson assumes the role of the Bemused Inquirer, puzzled by the fact that his own friends not only read detective stories but actually admit to enjoying them. Reading some of the more popular ones in an effort to discover the attraction, he finds Dorothy Sayers' *The Nine Tailors* much too long, Agatha Christie's work too trivial to read seriously, and Rex Stout's Nero Wolfe stories simply a rehash of the Sherlock Holmes formula. He confesses to a high impatience with all this nonsense, skipping a great deal as he reads and, in the case of *The Nine Tailors*, estimating that Conan Doyle could have finished off the whole business in about thirty pages.

This restless impatience with the detective story betrays one of Wilson's weaknesses as a critic of formula fiction, his failure to recognize the game-element that is basic to the conception of the mystery. It is not difficult, when he confesses to running through not only Sayers but Margery Allingham and Ngaio Marsh, to see why he finds them dull. Wilson's failure to understand this game-element as part of the basic purpose of the mystery would also result in his failure to recognize that in this type of story many of those long, often tedious, lists and descriptions, and those prolonged digressions from the main plot are a delight to the experienced reader, who recognizes their real purpose. The reader of a mystery is much like the baseball fan, who knows better than to fidget through those interminable arguments between manager and umpire, even though he suspects that most of this ritual by-play is staged.

Even more fundamental, though, is Wilson's lack of understanding of the essential nature of formula and convention. He sees the weight of tradition in the Sherlock Holmes stories, but continuation in later writers is to him mere imitation. The real principle, the one Wilson fails to recognize, is that when traditions become established and acceptable to later readers, they become conventions which are necessary for a viable relationship between author and reader, and hence a formulaic framework within which both feel comfortable. This is especially true in the Nero Wolfe stories: the readers are at home in the myth of Wolfe's routines and his prejudices and eccentricities, which are not, by the way, too different from those of the Holmes myth.

The fact is that Edmund Wilson, in spite of all his good qualities as a critic, did not know how to interpret popular fiction. He wrote a review of J.R.R. Tolkein's *The Lord of the Rings* which infuriates the Middle Earth folk as much as the "Who Cares...?" article does the mystery fan, in which, among other things, he called Tolkien's work a fairy story "somehow out of hand."[9]

One point needs re-emphasis here: there is no reason why any standard critical mode can not be applied to the interpretation of popular formula fiction, if the critic will remember that the attraction of a large reading public is the basic purpose of such stories and that, consequently, the critic ignores the reader/consumer only at the risk of fundamental misinterpretation. Many critics, accustomed to dealing only with "serious" fiction, may make the mistake Wilson made, of going directly to the text in the act of interpretation. A more fruitful approach to the criticism of the formula story is to look through the eyes of the author, who, in the process of creation, is viewing his text through the eyes of his projected reader. Such an approach could have restrained Edmund Wilson from plunging headlong into *The Nine Tailors* without reference to author or reader, and coming up with the judgement that this novel is a combination of a sort of textbook on campanology and church architecture with a cock-and-bull story about a woman who commits bigamy without knowing it.

Which brings us to the purpose of this book, to develop a theoretical base for a critical approach to the interpretation of the formula story, especially designed *for* the formula story. Such an approach should, and hopefully will, take into account the relationship between author and reader that determines such tacit agreements as the two axioms of formula fiction, the reader-knowledge convention, and the special messages and signals that pass between author and reader, all of which will be treated at greater length in the next three chapters.

Before going on, we should make it clear that the word "criticism" in this book is a synonym of *interpretation* , which in turn naturally brings up the whole business of teaching. We should not forget that just about all the principles of Process Criticism can be useful in the two main objectives of teaching the popular formula story: first, to raise perception from the level of "enjoyment-relaxation" to that of interpretation, and second, to develop a grasp of principle that the student can apply in the interpretation of all types of fiction.

Specifically, the chief concern of this book will be the criticism/ interpretation of the mystery, which includes the detective story. There are two reasons for such a delimitation. In the first place, mystery-detection is, by all odds, the most popular type of formula fiction and the one which has produced more serious study than any of the others. If evidence of this latter point is desired, it can be seen in Walter Albert's monumental bibliography of secondary sources in mystery-detective fiction, 731 closely printed pages of listings of bibliographies, encyclopedias, checklists, books, and articles.[10] The other reason is that mystery-detection is my own field of interest.

Sometimes by implication, and more often directly, we will be discussing several types of formula fiction, because the mystery (both detective and non-detective), the tale of espionage and of the supernatural, and the thriller have more formulaic elements in common than not; as we will see in Chapter 4, they share a structure that is generated by the Suspense Process. Thus we can not develop a critical theory of the mystery without discussing the functional elements in the others. As we have already seen, the nomenclature of the book-trade and even the academic setting tend to be confusing: the spy story may be practically all mystery, and many detective stories (the hard-boiled variety, for example) contain very little mystery but are stories of the head-on-collision type. To avoid confusion, however, we will continue to use the traditional designations: a mystery is "a fiction whose form and action are based on one or more artfully protracted questions,"[11] a detective story is a story in which the mystery is solved by a detective, and so on. We will also avoid the ambiguous term "thriller," and speak of the encounter story in which the thrust of the narrative is provided by the conflict or contest between two opposites. At the same time we must bear in mind that an author's purpose may change as the story progresses, causing it to shift from one kind of process to the other. The most usual is the shift from mystery to encounter, as the early mystery is solved (or partly so) and the motivation comes to be supplied by the conflict between menace and intended victim, as is the case with *The Exorcist* and *The Andromeda Strain*.

Here is the plan for the rest of this book. Chapter 2 will be an outline of the theoretical base for the process approach to the interpretation of formula fiction. Chapters 3 and 4 will develop this base in some detail, with respect to the actual working of the Suspense Process and the interrelationships of the components within the whole narrative structure. The next seven chapters will be analyses of an assortment of formula stories, for the purpose of showing how the theoretical base may be used in the practical business of interpretation. The final chapter will undertake to summarize the basic ideas of Process Criticism.

Chapter 2
Reading a Formula Story

The Suspense Process can be defined as what takes place between the reader and the book he is reading. It varies in terms of a great many elements, such as the experiential makeup of the reader, the circumstances of the reading, and the purpose of the novel, but it will, particularly in the case of a popular formula story, be marked by certain qualities and governed by certain functions that can be identified and described as the basis for an approach to the interpretation of formula fiction in general. The one thing we want to remember is that reading (again, especially in the case of the popular formula story) is a participatory business, or as, one writer puts it, "an act of imaginative co-operation between reader and novel."[1]

We will, then consider process as the juncture between reader and text, and will treat the three elements accordingly.

The Reader

Our model is based in part on the assumption of the reader-as-author and in part on the related notion that there is no such thing as an objective, culturally neutral reader. These two, taken together, should dispel the image of the reader as empty vessel into which the writer pours his narrative. "The reader may believe that he is completely receptive and uncritical," Joyce Cary says, "but in fact he is performing a highly active and complex creative act."[2]

One point on which traditionalists and "new new" critics agree is the conception of the reader who is also in his own way the author of the story. Thus Percy Lubbock: "The reader of a novel—by which I mean the critical reader—is himself a novelist."[3] And thus the structuralist position as stated by Jonathan Culler: "To read is to participate in the play of the text."[4] The conception should not seem fanciful to the serious student of the detective story. In that fiction, more than any other, the reader spins his own story while the printed one unfolds in his hands. He does his own sifting of clues, his own interrogation of suspects, his own search for hidden motives and patterns of conduct. He also, especially after a little experience, may learn not to trust his author too far, as when he wonders, for instance, why the writer has suddenly changed the subject and gone off into a new and different plot direction. And, of course, the writer of the mystery knows his readers will be doing all these things, with the result that the reader actually influences the text, as we pointed out in the discussion of our author's projection of his reader in Chapter 1.

The other feature that must be taken into account while we are addressing the primacy of the reader in the suspense process is the immediate influence of the culture; in all probability, there is greater evidence of cultural structuring in the formula story than in non-formula fiction. The reason should be obvious enough, considering that literary conventions are themselves expressions of the culture. It is the culture that determines the nature and acceptability of conventions, which in turn may be interpreted as specializations of one aspect of the culture.[5] Examples in the mystery are not hard to come by. Poe planted in "The Murders in the Rue Morgue" the device of the obtuse police, which persists as a convention right down to the most recent episode of "Murder, She Wrote." This is an example of *social* conditioning; the reader accepts the idea because it does not conflict with his own perceptions of the real world. Another convention introduced in "The Murders in the Rue Morgue" and still popular is the locked room, which illustrates a more essential aspect of our culture, the need for a secure world from which all unresolved paradoxes are eliminated.

In the preface to his translation of the eighteenth century novel featuring the Chinese master of detection, Judge Dee, Robert Van Gulik provides a first-class illustration of the influence of cultural shaping on the conventions of the formula story, listing five characteristics of Chinese detective fiction that are specifically contradictory to our western "rules" for the novel of detection: 1) In the Chinese story the criminal is fully introduced at the beginning, with an explanation of his motive; 2) The stories are filled with supernatural elements; 3) The narratives are freely interrupted by long poems, philosophical digressions, and full-length official documents; 4) They teem with characters, usually in the hundreds; 5) Descriptions of the punishment of the guilty party are lengthy and detailed. The differences are of course cultural. The eighteenth century Chinese reader, Van Gulik explains, loved the supernatural, enjoyed a leisurely, slow-paced existence, honored family relationships, and possessed a rigid sense of justice.[6]

Thus, the conditioning or cultural shaping of the reader manifests itself in the expectations of the reader and the purpose of the author. With respect to the reader of a formula story, the conditioning may result from any one or more of three factors, which really represent three types of reader-"readiness." First there is conditioning that arises in non-reading experience. The introduction of an anomalous element (such as a mysterious stranger) almost automatically stimulates tension, as does the corresponding situation in the real world. Or, conditioning may come from non-formula reading. A reader with experience in non-formula fiction will already be sensitized to an unexpected change of point of view, or to an extended period of peace and quiet in a situation in which trouble is obviously brewing, as a signal of suspense. Thirdly, conditioning arises from the reading of formula stories. The reader of mysteries soon learns, for example, to suspect any character who has had acting experience. There is considerable carry-over of "readiness" from the conditioning of one type of formula to another. When we discuss the signals of suspense will meet the encounter-story device of the Expendable S.O.B., who translates very readily into the Most Likely Victim familiar to mystery buffs.

We can be more specific with regard to the nature of the cultural shaping of the reader. It is an expression of, and also expresses itself in, two controls, a code of ethics and a level of acceptance.

The ethical system is implicit in the agreement between a writer and reader of a formula story, which attests that, by convention, the reader has a right to expect a satisfactory resolution. Such a contract is necessary to the generation of suspense, because with it a reader approaches the most hopeless narrative deadlock (Josephine Tey's *The Franchise Affair* comes to mind, or Eugene Burdick and Harvey Wheeler's *Fail-Safe*) with assurance that it will be solved, and this assurance keeps him turning pages. The ending may be defeat for the "sympathetic" character, or the culprit may escape punishment, but the reader must know the solution and feel that he has been treated fairly.

Most writers are scrupulous in bringing their stories to satisfying and acceptable conclusions: *The Franchise Affair* is resolved by the standard device of breaking one element in the paradox; *Fail-Safe* ends with the purposeful loss of New York City, but a nuclear holocaust is avoided. I think we can get a more exact test of the ethical concept by looking at two borderline cases.

Undoubtedly, many readers of Janwillem van de Wetering's *The Butterfly Hunter* were disappointed in the null ending of that story, especially if they took literally the advertisement of it as "a novel of suspense" on the dust-jacket. *The Butterfly Hunter* is the account of the efforts of the ambitious Eddy Sachs and his fellow conspirators to get their hands on a map that will lead them to a fabulous cache of buried Nazi gold. The quest takes them to Colombia, where they find and photograph the map, but there Eddy is killed (214). As he boards the plane to return to Europe, Eddy's partner discovers that the camera with the photograph has been stolen, and the reader never knows whether there really was any Nazi hoard (218). Now, if the critic seeks to decide whether such an ending is fair play, he must first look at the author's purpose and the manner in which that purpose can be seen in the author's handling of his readers. If the purpose is to develop the tension of Eddy's desire to find the gold versus the difficulty in locating and photographing the map, then the *partial* solution (Eddy's death) is acceptable, but not the final solution (the theft of the camera). But if the tension arises from Eddy's ambition in general and his view of the world as his oyster, then both solutions are acceptable and both within the ethical system. Another element enters the picture: van de Wetering is one of the more experimental writers, and the reader familiar with his earlier work should be listening to the Voice of Cognition, which tends to moderate the Voice of the Novel. So, of course, should the critic.

A more representative problem is the one in Reginald Hill's *A Clubbable Woman*. Early in that story the writer works a neat piece of cover-up by means of a switch of points of view, where a character named Connon collapses unconscious across the bed, whereupon the scene immediately switches to another situation (19). After a couple more changes the narrative view returns to Connon, who has regained consciousness to find his wife dead (23). It is more than 150 pages later that the reader is informed that Connon actually awoke much earlier than we had been led to believe (178). Agatha Christie was accused of this kind of breach of ethics in *The Murder of Roger Ackroyd*, but she had carefully covered her flanks by holding the point of view strictly with the guilty narrator, whereas Hill resorts to narrative hanky-panky.

Two points should not escape us. The first is the ethics of the Suspense Process as a product of culture. What should we say about William Marsh's locked-room story "The Bird House," with its multiple-choice ending (three solutions), or Frank Stockton's celebrated tossup story, "The Lady or the Tiger?" both of which represent conspicuous departures from the code? The persistence of convention as cultural product is most evident in the fact that neither of these innovations was imitated to any degree by later writers. "The Bird House," though occasionally anthologized, never became a prototype, and "The Lady or the Tiger?" continues to be a once-in-a-century curiosity, without having influenced the formula. The other point is the cruciality of the author's purpose for the critic undertaking the interpretation of fiction through examination of process. Dismissal of a story as trickery or a violation of the fair play convention on the evidence of the text alone is not enough; the critic must force himself into awareness of the author's relationship with his reader and develop the habit of looking at the story through the eyes of the author who is in turn viewing it through the eyes of his projected reader.

The other control of cultural shaping is what we are calling the level of acceptance, or the degree to which the reader participates in the reality of the story. Such a conception is by definition at the heart of the Suspense Process, because it is an expression of the element of caring, which is basic to the functional idea of suspense. Levels of acceptance are products of the culture, and as such they are subject to considerable conditioning. Evidence of the cultural nature of acceptance is often easy to recognize in theatre audiences: in the first year or so after Pearl Harbor, while apprehensions were still at high pitch in this country, movie-goers were known to scream "It's a Jap!" at the sudden appearance of any uniformed figure in a jungle movie. The low level of acceptance can be illustrated in the viewing of an old black and white silent film by a pseudo-sophisticated audience of undergraduates who consider it unspeakably silly. We should also take note of the fact that there are certain suspense themes that almost automatically assure a relatively high level of acceptance in contemporary western culture, like amnesia *(The Bourne Identity),* mindless menace *(Jaws, The Tower),* or the impossible-anomalous situation of the locked-room story.

We need to dwell a little on the obvious fact that level of acceptance is subject to considerable conditioning, for the reason that it affords a first-class example of the fashion in which an author manages his projected reader. Level of acceptance can be raised, for example, by injecting real-life elements into the story, like references to familiar landmarks and well-known personalities: we are more likely to care about the people trapped in the burning skyscraper if we know it is located in Manhattan not far from the World Trade Center *(The Tower),* or to sympathize with the harassed President if we recognize him as John F. Kennedy *(Fail-Safe).* Much better evidence of the writer's consciousness of his reader, however, is evident in the method by which a skillful writer can lead us to accept values we would ordinarily reject. Arthur Hailey does this with his little old lady stowaway in *Airport:* because we know her so well, our sympathies are with her; she becomes an excellent vehicle of suspense, because we know nothing bad can happen to her. Note how conditioning in this case starts with a cultural-formulaic foundation: in our fictional world bad things just do not happen to little old ladies who are smarter than the authorities.

We can see the relationship between the sense of ethics and the level of acceptance by examining the problem introduced in an exemplary mystery of the formal problem type, Josephine Tey's *The Franchise Affair,* a work we have cited earlier and will be using again in other connections. *The Franchise Affair* is built around an absolute contradiction of two equally untenable choices: either a) the young woman who charges that she was held prisoner and brutalized by the two older women is making up the whole story, including some corroborative details she could not possibly have known about if she were lying, or b) two women, whom the reader has been led to trust and respect, imprisoned and brutalized a fifteen-year-old. To propose Solution a) is to demand a level of acceptance far higher than most readers would permit, because it would ascribe to Betty Kane a clairvoyant knowledge of details of the interior of the Sharpe house, which she had never seen. Solution b), though, revealing the Sharpe sisters as brutes, would be a violation of the ethics of the formula, because it would convert the formula story to the mimetic mode. Thus, the tension generated by the paradox in *The Franchise Affair* is not so much between Betty Kane and the Sharpe sisters, or between Solutions a) and b) as between the author and her reader; the reader knows the problem will be solved (that is axiomatic) and the formula will be honored. The anticipation is based not so much on the ending of the story as on how the author works herself out of this one.

Thus culture generates the state of formulaic conditioning, the type of "readiness" we bring to the reading of a formula story. We will not accept a resort to the psychic as solution of a paradox (except in a tale of the supernatural), but neither will we accept a violation of the formula. Incidentally, the reader of *The Franchise Affair* will remember that it is the formula which prevails here, through the intervention of a venerable piece of conventional wisdom: When all the impossible has been eliminated, whatever remains, no matter how improbable, must be the truth.[7]

Since conditioning is a product experience, the effect of this type of "readiness" will vary with the reader, in terms of his previous experience of the formula. Thus a reader without earlier acquaintance may have an entirely different reaction from that of a veteran fan as a result of a different predisposition. A first-time reader of Raymond Chandler, for example usually sees only "realism" and misses the evocation of the heroic code in *The Long Goodbye*. The difference, though, is chiefly one of nature rather than degree; strong tensions may result during reading by the inexperienced reader, but created by a different set of factors. This condition characteristically changes with experience.

The formulaic conditioning of a reader serves to intensify the Suspense Process in two ways. First, it is produced by the novel's own adherence to formula, as when the reader is supplied with some important knowledge not shared with the characters in the story, with the result that he participates as a privileged insider capable of passing judgements superior to those of the characters. Or, suspense may be heightened by the author's liberal use of the conventions of the formula story, such as the detective's struggle to recover "something at the back of his mind," or the garrulous fellow-passenger who seats himself next to the secret agent on a train. Writers will often capitalize on both of these types of conditioning by introducing some familiar old cliche, like the corpse whose hands have been removed, to give the reader an opportunity to feel superior.

As a result of this conditioning, the reader can approach the story with two kinds of confidence, both of them so firm as to constitute axioms of the Suspense Process. The first is that, in a formula story, everything is likely to be important, or to use the language of Formalist criticism, there are no "free motifs" in a formula story.[8] It should be noted that the generalization applies only to the specific instance at hand: for *this* reader, in *this* novel, all motifs are "bound". The second axiom is one we have already discussed, that a formula story will always have a resolution. Both of these are necessary to the successful generation of suspense, partly because they contribute to the creation of tension between author and reader, and partly because they impose discipline upon the game by keeping it in bounds.

The Process

We will begin this discussion of the Suspense Process with the reminder that the purpose of reading a formula story is essentially different from that of a non-formula one. I think we can recognize the difference by means of analogy: Reading a formula novel the first time is very much like *re-reading* a non-formula novel.

Katherine Lever says some interesting things about what happens when we re-read a good novel like *Pride and Prejudice*. Art, she points out, has one advantage over life: we can re-experience it. Re-reading *Pride and Prejudice*, we are not motivated primarily by the need to learn how it turns out; we know, for example, that Elizabeth and Darcy will marry. Nevertheless, says Lever, "with each re-reading of a good novel, we gain in appreciation and insight." Moreover, the tension created by our foreknowledge, added to the inevitability of the conclusion, creates "more absorbing reading than simple curiosity." Then, possessing knowledge that characters do not have, we react as we read, with advice like "Don't do it," "Listen to him!" and the like.[9] Notice how closely her description of re-reading parallels what we have been saying about formulaic conditioning and convention, reader-knowledge and reader-participation.

Consider, first, her premise regarding inevitability of conclusion, which reminds us of those two aspects of reader-readiness, the code of ethics in the formula story and the axiomatic guarantee that the story will have a resolution. Actually, the reader of the formula novel has the best of both worlds, enjoying the security of foreknowledge and, at the same time, the suspended outcome. "We know that the hero or heroine will be saved in some way," says Cawelti, "because he always is."[10] The sense of security comes from the "we know" part, and the excitement of anticipation from the "in some way."

The tension created by foreknowledge, says Lever, generates a better reading than does simple curiosity. Foreknowledge is basic to successful suspense. What keeps the reader turning pages is not so much what he wants to find out as what he already knows, as a result of those messages and signals transmitted to him by the author.

This foreknowledge, finally, actively involves the reader in the story, in Lever's example of the re-reading of *Pride and Prejudice*, causing reactions like "Don't do it!" inwardly addressed to the characters. The same thing happens in a popular situation, as when the 1940s movie-goer was stimulated to scream "It's a Jap!" or, reading a formula novel we chuckle, "That's what you think" to a character who says, "I know I'm going to be perfectly safe here."

This combination of recognitions and anticipations is the essence of the Suspense Process in the formula story. The comfortable-old-shoe effect joins with the excitement of the new situation, and the reader moves through the story with certain expectations clearly understood by himself and the author, with the result that the reader feels at home in the story, as if he were a participant. This essential nature must be understood by the critic, who, if he misses it, runs the risk of making a fool of himself as did Edmund Wilson with those *New Yorker* columns.

Before moving on to the operation of the process, we must take a look at the instruments that condition it, the game-element, delay, and shock.

Of these three, the game-element has the most substance, because it is indigenous in suspense in the formula story. The process that keeps a sports fan fixed in front of a TV screen for three straight hours on a Sunday afternoon is much like the one that keeps him turning pages through a novel: he does it because he cares. His caring, in the one instance, may result from loyalty, or from knowledge of the closely matched strengths of opponents, or from recognition of the cruciality of this particular game. If it is to be a continued caring, though, he will learn to analyze relative strengths and weaknesses, come to know the eccentricities of individual players, and learn to anticipate and appreciate certain tactics. He will also develop a respect for the rules and traditions of the game as essentials to enjoyment:

the purpose is not just to play it, but to do it in a certain way. Those rules perform much the same function as the conventions of the formula story: cheating on the part of the writer (withholding essential information from a mystery reader, for example) dampens suspense in the same way as having twelve players on the field does in a football game.

What about the game-element in a story where one protagonist is so far superior as to eliminate all suspense over the outcome, as in the case of a super-hero like James Bond? Umberto Eco draws a clever parallel between a Bond story and a game between the Harlem Globetrotters and the local team. Such a game will be a sellout, but not because of any question of who will win. "The pleasure," says Eco, "lies in watching the trained virtuosity with which [the Globetrotters] defer the final moment, with what ingenious deviations they reconfirm the foregone conclusion, with what trickeries they make rings around their opponents."[11]

Some critics speak of delay as if it depended, in the mystery story, only upon the exercise of impediment. Thus Roland Barthes in the section of *S/Z* entitled "Delay" lists five "dilatory morphemes": the snare, equivocation, the partial answer, the suspended answer, and jamming, used "to *arrest* the enigma, to keep it open."[12] In somewhat more satisfying detail Dennis Porter also lists five: 1. peripeteia, the reversal, which is a deflection from progress; 2. the antidetective or criminal, who blocks the advance toward resolution; 3. the eccentricities of the main characters, such as the taciturn Great Detective and the garrulous assistant; 4. the episodes themselves; and 5. assorted verbal elements, such as extended descriptive passages.[13] In a recent interview John Mortimer offers a piece of aphoristic advice to writers who want to achieve suspense: "Make them laugh; make them cry; make them wait."[14] The sequence is important; an author is not going to make anybody wait until he has made them laugh or cry, that is, made them care. In Chapter 4 we will discuss a structural device that induces delay by serving the same purpose as the out-of-bounds marker on a game field and keeps the plot from running away with itself. Plausible delay, especially in the mystery, is built into the story.

Of the third instrument, shock, we need at this point to say that it is a device which can promote suspense only if used in moderation. That shattering bomb-blast early in Fleming's *Casino Royale*, for which the reader is completely unprepared, does provide a few pages of excitement, but it is Bond's deliberately paced gambling contest with LeChiffre a little later that really holds a reader's attention.

The Suspense Process is conditioned by two elements, the Two Voices and the Lecturer Beside the Screen. During the Act of reading we are listening, simultaneously, to the Voice of the Novel and the Voice of Cognition. The Voice of the Novel sometimes speaks dramatically, as it does in the Philo Vance stories of S.S. Van Dine, but more often it speaks through the planted information, the hints and suggestions, even the structure of the story. The Voice of the Novel keeps saying things like, This is an absolute paradox, for which there is no solution except one that will deny our basic assumptions about the orderly universe. It has been reinforced, during the history of the detective story, by some distinguished antecedents, such as a statement in almost every Holmes story that "I can not recall any case which presented more singular features," or "I think, Watson, that of all our cases we have had none more fantastic than this."

The Voice of Cognition is the one that tells us there is no such thing as absolute paradox, especially not in a formula story. This is the voice that is the product of cultural shaping, specifically conditioned by its earlier experience with formula fiction. It develops in two ways: it tends to insulate the reader against the "hype" that often characterizes the Voice of the Novel, and it also produces a comfortable sense of *deja vu* as the reader begins to feel at home within the familiar shape of the formula.

We need to give special attention to the Voice of Cognition as the essence of the whole concept of process, the dynamic relationship between reader and text. It is, as we have said, a result of cultural conditioning, specifically that part seen in literary formulas, and it encompasses such concepts as ethics, level of acceptance, and some others we will be discussing later. Like most reading skills, it can be strengthened through experience and socialization.

Almost any reader who sticks with a formula long enough will develop a feel for the genre that will heighten his capacity for enjoyment, but he will not experience the highest level of participation until he develops real appreciation, that is, an ability to experience with his author the act of creation. "To perceive," says Dewey, "a beholder must *create* his own experience. And this creation must include relations comparable to those which the original producer underwent."[15] The somnolent reader, too lazy or unresponsive to join in the work of creation, is not likely to attain the status of critic or fan.

Nor does the Voice of Cognition in a given reader reach maximum strength in isolation. Like fans of every stripe, detection addicts are gregarious and love to exchange views with their fellows who enjoy similar tastes. The sense of fraternity is strong among them, as can be seen in a reading of the Letters columns in the early issues of *The Armchair Detective*, where the impression is one of written conversation among people who love to swap ideas with each other especially in correcting mistakes and supplying each other's lack of knowledge. The sense of fraternity among detective story fans became a sort of slogan when *TAD* was a few years older and it appeared to some of them that the journal was losing its fanzine orientation and becoming too academic; they complained of the "loss of intimacy" and absence of the "fraternal feeling" that had marked the first few years of *TAD* [16] The same spirit was recognized by a commentator who characterized another journal as "more genial and affectionate than scholarly."[17] Two facts need to be borne in mind here. First, many of the non-academic fans who correspond with these journals are excellent scholars in their hobby, with prodigious knowledge of novels, authors, and publications, and with totally admirable insistence upon strict accuracy of detail. The other is the degree of ego-satisfaction involved in these participations, which is much like that state created by the privileged information supplied to reader by author, giving him a feeling of superiority over the characters, a feeling that translates easily into the enjoyment of knowledgeable superiority over one's fellow fans, a good-natured egotism that is both affectionate and playfully aggressive.

Let it be remembered that the academics who do research in the field of mystery-detective fiction and write for the journals are also fans, who have intellectualized their love of the genre. In them, the Voice of Cognition is better organized and has firmer theoretical support than in the recreational fan, but the game-element is just as strong, producing the same kind of geniality and absence of abrasiveness as that enjoyed by their non-academic colleagues and contributing to the comraderie often remarked in the Mystery-Detection Caucus of the Popular Culture Association.

The Voice of Cognition is also a powerful generator of suspense. One level of tension is produced by the Voice of the Novel, in the workings of plot, of the variety of atmospheric effects, and the pleasurable combination of resolution and surprise. Another is that of the Voice of Cognition, which we have compared to the experience of re-reading a non-formula story, with the feelings of recall and recognition, the perception of signals *as* signals. There is still a third level, created by the tension between the Two Voices, that opens a whole new dimension of interpretation.

Suspense, then, is basically the product of tensions created by the process, such as the competition between the Two Voices. We must not forget, however, that, especially when the formula is most influential, some highly effective suspense is brought about by tensions between reader and author. It is time now to introduce one of the leading figures in the formula novel, the Lecturer Beside the Screen. We can picture the story as a movie unfolding before us; to one side of the screen, however, stands the Lecturer, who periodically comments on the story . He keeps reminding us that in a formula story anything is likely to be important and offers such advice as, "Listen to what he is saying. Where have you heard that before?" The Lecturer shares some of the qualities of reader and some of author, and he speaks with the Voice of Cognition and also that of the novel. It is the Lecturer who passes along the messages and makes those signals that are private to the experienced reader and will pass largely unrecognized by the uninitiated. He is not always reliable; especially in the detective story, he may assume the role of con artist, purposefully and skillfully misdirecting us, dragging in red herrings, feeding us malarkey. Most especially, though, he is the force that keeps us turning pages.

This is why we are calling the Suspense Process a dynamic relationship between reader and text. Its clearest expression lies in the quality we designate as reader-knowledge. Successful suspense, remember, is dependent not nearly so much upon delay as upon thrust, not so much on what the reader is anxious to find out as on what he already knows. David Daiches puts it this way: "True suspense is not dependent on ignorance of the eventual outcome but on waiting for the inevitable to happen,"[18] which re-states the argument of Eco's game analogy. We will have a great deal more to say about reader-knowledge in the next chapter, but meanwhile there are two things to keep in mind. The first is that when we speak of reader-knowledge we are speaking of information or insight that is not shared by some or any of the characters in the story; it is this privileged state which not only makes the reader a participant but makes him care, thus producing tension. The effect is especially evident in the "inverted" story of detection, where the reader sees the crime committed and may even know the motive; the suspense is generated for him as he watches the detectives try to discover what he already knows, while he whispers, "That's it! You're headed in the right direction," or "Oh, no, not him, Stupid!" The other thing is that reader-knowledge in the mystery may take the form of questions rather than information, as the reader is able to perceive possibilities that do not occur to the characters, or to re-state questions and recognize the real significance of clues.

Tension in a suspenseful story is generated in one or more of several ways. Ordinarily, we think of it as something that occurs only between the antagonists, the menace and the victim or the detective and the guilty one. It can also result from the conflict between the major characters in the story and that out-of bounds marker that provides the discipline of the plot. It achieves an extra dimension when it is produced by the contest between writer and reader, in those pleasant dichotomies generated by the Two Voices and the Lecturer.

There are two important things to remember about the whole idea of process in the interpretation of formula fiction. The first is that process will itself become formulaic as messages, signals, and structures become conventionalized. The other is that, as a result of this conventionalization, writers have an additional opportunity for the creation of suspense. We know that the hero will be saved, as Cawelti says, because he always *is* saved. Here Cawelti suggests that other possibility, the one Alfred Hitchcock used effectively, that maybe, just this once, the hero will be dumped. In a mimetic story, Cawelti points out, the effect would not be nearly so powerful because of the absence of the pressure of formula.[19]

The Text

Now, after attempting to develop an understanding of the role of the reader and the nature of the process, we are ready to turn to the novel itself. The oblique approach is essential to the critic of popular fiction who seeks to interpret a story in terms of purpose. Other critics may view texts directly in the light of their own literary values, but the popular culturist must look at the text through the eyes of the intended reader, because it is the reader who determines the book's popularity and thus its level of success.

In Chapter 4 we will explore the popular formula novel in terms of its structure, by which we mean not just the framework of the story but all those arrangements of parts within the whole and the relationships between the parts and the whole, as well as among the parts themselves. As far as the framework of the formula story is concerned, its shape is determined far more by convention than by genre or theme, because convention by nature represents that practical, workable agreement within which both author and reader are comfortable.

Convention, as a matter of fact, lays a heavier hand on the framework of the story than does reality as reflected in the power of modern technology. When John Gardner published his neo-Bond story *License Renewed* in 1981, the image of James Bond as infallible super-hero had become too firmly set to be modified. Part of the narrative problem is that the high-tech equipment available to Bond ought to result in resolution after forty or fifty pages, but the formula precludes early success in a full-length novel. Conan Doyle faced substantially the same problem with Sherlock Holmes and solved it, awkwardly in three of the novels, by means of those long, digressive stories-within-the-stories. Gardner's solution is a combination of accident and coincidence. Having hidden a "bug" in Murik's study, Bond is getting enough information to reveal all he is seeking (and, consequently, to finish his job much too quickly), and so his receiver conveniently fails at the worst possible moment (98-9). Now Bond is himself in real jeopardy but decides not to trigger his ingenious pen-alarm that will radio for help; so, at the crucial point, most in need of rescue, he discovers he has lost his pen (152). Readers of a non-formula story would not tolerate such blatant implausibility, but convention (which represents the reader's acculturation) supersedes not only reality but even the myth of Bond's invulnerability.

It is not surprising, then, that the Suspense Process determines structure, even to the extent that there is a common structure integral in the genres we are discussing, mystery and encounter. In Chapter 4 we will go into some detail regarding the four phases or states integral in the detective story, the "straight" mystery, the spy story, the ghost story, and the encounter story. Any fiction controlled by the Suspense

Process will follow the general outlines of the phases of cumulation, postponement, alternation, and potentiality.

The process also determines the employment of several components of the formula story (See Chapters 3 and 4), including those promissory plants that sustain the reader's participation, messages inherent in the plot that promise future development. These messages, as we will see, are sometimes intended for the reader to remember and sometimes for him to forget. In the mystery, these plants may appear as standard clues, concealed clues, or camouflaged clues. Those stimuli we are calling signals are different from messages in the sense that they serve only as communication and need not directly influence the development of the plot. A familiar example is the reiterated statement of the exact time, which induces tensions in the reader whether or not it is germane to the plot. Another structural feature of the process is the discipline we referred to earlier as the out-of-bounds marker, the exclusion of alternatives that keeps the story from running away with itself.

In Chapter 4 we will also have more to say about the method of development of the suspense plot. The usual formula is the pattern of obstacle-progress-obstacle, which is applicable in both the mystery and the encounter story. There is another, however, common in the tale of supernatural and occasionally in other types, the organization-disorientation-disorganization pattern.

We can find the clearest evidence of the Suspense Process in the selection of materials used, including all those available incidents. situations, relationships and even language. For this reason, the very fact that *something is there* attracts attention, arouses curiosity, raises questions, builds tensions. Fletcher Knebel uses the principle effectively in his *Night of Camp David:* the puzzlement created by the erratic behavior of the President is interrupted by a switch to an apparently irrelevant scene, the meeting of a committee directing a project called "CACTUS" (Command and Control, The Ultimate System), who are working out policies for the role of top government officials in decision-making regarding the use of nuclear weapons (91). A mild shock resulting from the sudden interruption of the narrative is usually guaranteed to raise the reader's level of interest, but Knebel works an extra degree of tension with a skillful promissory plant, a suggestion of the awesome possibility of an insane president. The plant is especially effective because, as the story progresses, the reader will keep going back to take another look at CACTUS and will find himself increasingly involved in the story as the reality of CACTUS evolves.

Finally, it is basic to an understanding of the Suspense Process that the nature of the problem (the mystery to be solved or the encounter to be decided) is considerably more important to structure and the selection of techniques than are formal genre and theme. Earlier, in discussing formulaic conditioning, we used Josephine Tey's *The Franchise Affair* to illustrate the way in which formula dominates resolution. We can also demonstrate the precedence of problem over genre and theme by comparing that story with Tey's *Miss Pym Disposes*, which belongs in the same genre and even shares the same theme but is structured quite differently. Both novels develop the theme of the inadequacy of reason. After the failure of her "disposing," Miss Pym decides that as a psychologist she would make a good French teacher (174); in *The Franchise Affair*, reason works only up to a point, at which the solution is chiefly by chance. They also share the nominal genre of mystery. The differences in structuring develop mainly out of the difference in the problem. The crime is delayed until three quarters of the way through *Miss Pym;* until then, the reader's interest is maintained by several devices, such as minor mysteries, hints and suggestions, tensions among the characters. In *Franchise*, the impossible problem dominates the story from the first; the technique is to hold the reader by re-definition, re-emphasis of the impossibility of solution, while hinting at and suggesting approaches to it. To anticipate a figure we will employ later Tey spends most of the length of *Miss Pym* rolling a snowball; she starts peeling the onion on almost the first page of *Franchise*.

At several points in this chapter we have referred to formulaic conditioning, that aspect of cultural readiness brought to the reading of a formula story by a reader having earlier experience with such stories. But what about the reader without such experience, who picks up a formulaic mystery after having read only non-formula fiction? Obviously such a reader can be as thoroughly hooked as a veteran can, but with a difference. He will, if the story is well done, enjoy the mystification and the excitement. He will hear the Voice of the Novel, but will miss the Voice of Cognition. He will miss all those gestures, facial expressions, and inflections of the Lecturer Beside the Screen, and will fail to recognize many or most of the conventionalized signals. He is, in that sense, *reading a different story* from the one read by the long-time fan. If he reads another one, this will change, and he will come to see those stories in a decidedly different light from that of the first one. It is in this way that reader and text really condition each other.

This reciprocal conditioning is only one example of the inter-relatedness and mutuality in the process approach to interpretation. Note, for example, the number of cases in which the relationship between two elements can be best stated in terms of "influences/is influenced by," such as process and structure, and caring and tension. Note too the indications that it is impossible to discuss level of acceptance without the code of ethics, or structure without the formulaic axioms and the Voice of the Novel, or the level of acceptance without the Lecturer Beside the Screen and the out-of-bounds marker.

Chapter 3*
The Dynamics of Suspense

In this chapter we will consider the Suspense Process from the viewpoint of the author, who, as tactician and strategist, selects and organizes his narrative materials in such fashion as to sustain his readers' participation in the story. We have already met him in his role as Lecturer Beside the Screen, who keeps us hooked by means of hints, information, and suggestions. Generally, a successful producer of formula fiction must possess two qualities: a consciousness of his readers and of the formula within which he is working; and a faculty for inventiveness and ingenuity. Both are essential to the best possible exploitation of the opportunities of formulaic writing. Cawelti puts it this way: "...All cultural products contain a mixture of two kinds of elements: conventions and inventions." Conventions are those components familiar to author and readers, such as stereotypes and favorite plots. The inventions are the fresh elements imagined by the author, like new characters and situations.[1] Toward the end of this chapter we will see how one skilled writer, Robert Ludlum, can blend the two qualities in such a way as to practically insure maximum reader-involvement.

First we need to clarify the nature of invention by distinguishing between *suspense* and *shock*. Alfred Hitchcock, the master of suspense on the screen, illustrates the difference in this example: The Board of Directors is holding a meeting, ignorant of the fact that a time-bomb is planted under the table around which they are seated. If the bomb explodes, shattering the room and killing everybody in it, that, says Hitchcock, is *shock*. Suppose, though, that the camera recording the story periodically cuts away from the discussion and closes in on the timing device as it moves from 8:08 to 8:12 to 8:14, that is *suspense*.[2] The illustration is admirable, because it reminds

*An earlier version of this chapter appeared in *Symbiosis* edited by Ray B. Browne, Bowling Green State University Popular Press.

us that there are three elements involved in successful suspense, not just one. First, there is the impending menace, the bomb, which is the reason for telling the story in the first place. Note, too, that the formulaic axiom implies a kind of guarantee that the writer will do something with that bomb. Second, there is the ticking clock, the time-element that speaks with the Voice of the Novel and triggers the sense of impending crisis. Finally, and most important, there is the moving camera, which is essential to the Suspense Process, because its shifting perspective assures the viewer that something is going to happen, supplies him with an insight not shared by the board members around the table, and thus makes him a participant in the narrative. Not only that: the very act of repeatedly going back to the bomb prompts the viewer to ask, "Why is he doing this?" thus invoking the Voice of Cognition, which tells him that the author is tacitly keeping his options open. Something may yet happen prevent that explosion.

Notice that a definition of suspense that goes no further than the bomb may neglect a lot of good suspenseful story-telling, because it limits the process to dependence on simple menace. To stop with the clock is almost as unsatisfactory, because it limits the viewer's interest to that of non-participating onlooker. The moving camera is the promise, the signal that not only asks the viewer, "How do you think I can work this out?" but makes him a privileged insider, so that when the chairman of the board solemnly announces that the members are facing the best year in the history of the corporation, the reader is moved to comment, "That's what you think."

The principle is basic: skillfully managed prolongation intensifies pleasure. As Dennis Porter says, "... With mere progression there is simply a rush to the pleasure of a denouement that turns out to offer no pleasure at all."[3]

For catching and holding the reader's attention the author has access to four operational principles or types of reader-readiness.

The first of these, and probably the most familiar, is the principle of *focus*, that is location, direction, or specification. The strategy is most clearly seen in the handling of the camera, as it selects the Solitary Figure out of a crowd, closes in on him, follows him around the room and stays with him as he leaves. The Voice of the Novel is telling us, "Watch this person. He is important," and the Voice of Cognition, "The camera never wastes time. Of course he's important."

The tactic is most evident in a spatial situation, as when the narrator of Cornell Woolrich's *Rear Window* moves his eyes over that array of windows facing his, giving sketchy descriptions of each, until he focuses on one and expends so much detail on it that the reader can not escape the impression that this is *the* rear window of the title (3-4). The same effect can be achieved in a temporal frame by repeatedly focusing on the exact time or date, as Frederick Forsyth does very successfully in *The Day of the Jackal*, with his reiterated reminders, "The time was 7:55" and "The date was August 22." As we will note in the discussion of messages and signals, the exact time may or may not be material to the narrative, but the very fact of its being singled out catches our attention.

The second principle is that of *interruption*, departure, or contrast. When a character has just finished saying, "Now here is exactly what I plan to do," and the camera switches to something else, the viewer feels an irritation that produces tension and consequently suspense. In a mystery novel the device is most easily recognized in the sudden change of scene or point of view, but it can be more subtly effective in a change of pace or tempo. The principle is familiar to hunters, who know that any kind of change catches attention; the narrator of *Rear Window* learns to sit very still because, as he says "Motion attracts" (7). The principle of interruption has come to be a staple of television drama as a result of that godsend to suspense, the commercial, which has replaced the asterisk effect of the old erotic novel.

Intimation, or indirection, deserves special attention, because it is more familiar to mystery fans than to any other readers. Its obvious manifestation is in the use of suggestions, hints, and, in the detective story, clues. Poe introduces the device early in "The Murders in the Rue Morgue," when he describes the residence of the narrator and Dupin as "a time-eaten and grotesque mansion, long deserted through superstitions into which we did not inquire..." (165-6). The reader does not need to inquire; he gets the message. So does he when he reads at the end of Chapter Three of *The Exorcist,* "By midnight, all in the house were asleep. There were no disturbances. That night" (60). The promise in those last two words is a clear guarantee. So is the name of the boat the narrator in *Rebecca* discovers on the little beach so closely associated with the drowned Rebecca: "Je Reviens— I come back" (181). In the tale of detection these hints are sometimes clues; in the non-detective mystery they are planted stimuli of suspense. We should also mention the technique of *indirection*, because it is more common to the mystery than to the encounter story. Sometimes, through a fairly extended passage, the reader is unable to determine whether or not progress is taking place, whether the dynamic is mystification or analysis, as for example Chapters 4 and 5 of Len Deighton's *The Ipcress File;* during that passage the author moves the action right along, but without any indication whether he is rolling a snowball or peeling an onion.

The fastest and most effective method of drawing the reader into the story is the principle of *confidentiality,* whereby he is made privy to information not shared by the characters themselves. This strategy is the real dynamic of the Hitchcock example; tension is heightened for the viewer by the fact of his superiority over the board members innocently unaware of the bomb at their feet. The power of the device to generate suspense is generously illustrated in that extended passage in *Rebecca* following the narrator's decision to appear at the fancy dress ball in a costume that will make her look strikingly like the late Rebecca, which, as the reader knows but the narrator does not, is absolutely the worst possible thing for her to do. When she in innocent exhuberance tells two family friends "You won't know me...you will both get the shock of your lives" (246), the sympathetic reader is sure to cringe, as he will later when she laughingly asks her maid, "Oh, Clarice, what will Mr. de Winter say?" (253) One thing the reader will find it impossible to do from now on is to maintain an air of disinterest; he is in the story, whether his response is "Hoo boy, are you going to find out!" or "Will you please for heaven's sake just shut up!"

The reader's response to any of these strategies is of course regulated by his cultural conditioning, especially in regard to his previous experience of literature. Almost anybody's attention will be held, if only momentarily, by an unexpected interruption of pace or mood, but only an experienced fan may catch the fine nuances of an extended metaphor.

We must bear in mind that the application of all these principles is more functional than substantive. Quite often, the thing that catches our attention is not so much the presence of something in the story as what the author is doing with it. Process itself, as we will have many occasions to see during this discussion, conveys meaning. The pace of a story, for example, may be mildly exciting as it gallops or crawls along, but the surest stimulant to suspense is a sudden change of pace, causing us to look toward our author and ask, Why this? All of the operational principles, especially confidentiality, are instrumental in the special author-reader relationship in the formula story; the reader tends to watch the writer more closely than in other fiction, and the writer consequently tends to feed his audience more information and direction.

Those narrative elements that serve as stimuli to suspense, making the reader care and keeping him hooked, may be classed as "messages" and "signals." They are both used as promissory plants, which an author drops along the way and which carry the assurance that something is likely to happen as a result of each one. When we speak of messages we mean those elements that have content in itself germane to the plot, like the knowledge of that bomb under the table in Hitchcock's definition. Signals, on the other hand, may or may not be plot elements, their real function being that they serve as triggers of the reader's interest, like the moving camera in the Hitchcock story. Either may be a person, an object, a situation, or a relationship. As is the case with so many of the suspense phenomena, their effectiveness depends not so much upon form as upon function. Quite often, the method of telling is more important than the story told.

To illustrate: reiterated statements of the exact time (using the principle of focus) may be messages or signals. The statement of times in a story can be a real message, as it is in Cornell Woolrich's "Three O'Clock" where the helpless protagonist watches the alarm clock connected to the box of explosives at his feet creep minute by minute toward the fateful hour. In many tales of detection the exact time (sometimes the agonizingly split second) is basic to solution and hence a genuine message. Occasionally, though, these statements serve only as signals. There is an example in a passage in *The Exorcist* (115-18) where the reader should find himself bemused by a succession of statements, "They left the house at precisely 6:18 P.M.," "Then at 9:28, the front door-bell rang," and pages later, "At 11:46, Chris answered the phone." The reader can hardly miss the point because of the marked change the statements represent, and he should feel his level of alertness rise. Sure enough, the phone call announces that a murder has taken place. These emphatic references to exact moments can become guaranteed hooks, but the device is in this case a signal, because the time-element is not pertinent to the murder. S.S. Van Dine recognized the signal-value of exact time, sub-heading his chapters "Tuesday, September 11; 9:30 A.M." and the like, but those impressively exact times and dates almost never turn out to be clues, though they do effectively serve the purpose of keeping us attentive.

Almost any mystery story will contain a number of promissory plants that serve as messages. Eric Ambler uses the dependable promise of sexual development in *Journey Into Fear* as a very beautiful young woman makes repeated assertions of her interest in the protagonist; the reader follows closely because he knows an author seldom introduces such an element without giving it some kind of development (80,92). In the detective story, the clue is almost always a message, like the grey Plymouth Marlowe sees following him in Chandler's *The Big Sleep* (149-50). Again, however, the mere presence of a message may or may not be significant in a story, depending upon the way the author handles it. Ambler and Chandler make effective use of the elements just mentioned by periodically strengthening them through the process of reinforcement via re-introduction frequently enough to maintain the reader's curiosity. Fletcher Knebel uses the device on a larger scale in *The Night of Camp David* by unexpectedly abandoning the main plot unfolding in Washington and switching to an apparently unrelated scene on a ranch in Texas (Ch.8). After this happens twice, the reader can hardly avoid asking "What's going on?" and finding his attention divided between the unfolding story in Washington and whatever is so important out there in Texas. Moreover, the message, to be meaningful in the Suspense Process, must carry a promise: something is bound to come of this.

What we are calling *messages*, then, are those elements communicated by author to reader that supply knowledge substantive to the plot and not generally shared with the people in the story. *Signals* are also a kind of communication, but they have two special qualities: their own narrative content has an insignificant bearing on the outcome of the story, or none at all, and most of them have become conventions of the Suspense Process and consequently also serve as automatic triggers of reader interest.

A good illustration of both qualities can be seen in a familiar signal, the social-event-as-harbinger-of-crisis. Just let the mother in a menaced household announce, "I'm having a few friends in to dinner tomorrow evening," and the reader can brace himself for all hell to break loose. It happens in *Jaws;* after a week-end free of shark-attacks Ellen Brody, the wife of the chief of police in Amity, decides to give a small dinner party and does so in spite of her husband's uneasiness (125). Readers of *Jaws* will remember the outcome, which almost shatters the Brodys' marriage. The same thing happens in *The Exorcist;* after a short period or respite from the supernatural manifestations that have centered around little Regan, her mother hosts a dinner at her home, an event which, unsurprisingly, is broken up by the most hideous manifestation to date (56, 73). Almost the same thing happens in Peter Straub's *Ghost Story* (290, 329). Then, of course, there is the classic example, the fancy dress ball in *Rebecca*: the reader, already uneasy over the peril he sees surrounding the innocent narrator, may feel real concern at the suggestion to revive the Manderley fancy dress ball. This occasion, you will recall, is the one at which the young wife innocently appears in Rebecca's old costume and blows the family secret wide open.

Evidently a fairly complex chain of associations establishes a convention like this one. On the face of it there appears no harm in a pleasant little social gathering as a release from tensions. The reader, however, may feel some concern over the anomaly of a party in the midst of menace and terror, especially if he remembers the unfortunate attempts of Belshazzar and Lady Macbeth. If, however, after reading *Rebecca* and *The Exorcist* he hears the father in *Ghost Story* remark, "We're going to give a party," he can not miss the promise in the signal. We, of course, must not overlook the fact that in none of these cases is the social event germane to the plot itself. Like the Solitary Figure and the Exact Time, its effectiveness lies in its role as pure signal.

In addition to these three, here is a representative list of conventionalized signals:

The Expendable S.O.B. is the convention of a character on the "sympathetic" side who makes a nuisance of himself and almost automatically becomes a victim of the menace. The reader is almost certain to spot the role of J. Paul Norris in Stern's *The Tower*. One of those trapped in the burning skyscraper, Norris makes matters worse by complaining about the way the situation is being handled; finally he steals the elevator that might have saved a number of people, and is immediately incinerated (188, 203). Much the same thing happens to the degenerate family friend Dennings in *The Exorcist*, who becomes the first victim of the demon (118). So also with Hooper, the naturalist in *Jaws* who almost breaks up the Brody's home and is subsequently eaten by the great white shark (288). If we need further confirmation of this one, we should remember that Hooper in the movie version is converted to a nice guy and emerges from the crisis uneaten. The reader of the detective story should be able to recognize this conventional signal in the early pages of almost any traditional murder mystery, where there is no question who is going to be the first victim of the killer.

Excessive Detail in a story is a stimulant of suspense only when it signals the reader that something important is about to happen, by means of a flood of information that is essentially irrelevant to the plot. There is a representative example in *The Ipcress File*, where the narrator pauses to give a meticulous inventory of preparations for his next campaign: exact numbers of suits, dark shirts and white ones, ties, socks, underwear, shoes, razor, shaving cream, blades, comb, and other accessories (154), most of which have no bearing on the progress of the narrative but are bound to stimulate a reaction from the Voice of Cognition.

Fool to Worry: This device is usually more obvious, because of the unconcealed irony. When, early in his search in Buchan's *The Thirty-Nine Steps*, Richard Hannay remarks, "It was the same jolly clear spring weather and I simply could not contrive to feel careworn" (33), the reader senses the same kind of anomaly as the one experienced in the case of the Social Event in Peril: here is a promise of something about to happen.

The Gabby Fellow-Passenger, really a specialization of the Solitary Figure, seems to be most useful in the spy story. The situation is that of the secret agent who takes his seat on a bus or plane and is immediately engaged in conversation by a garrulous neighbor. Now the reader knows, especially if he has read Ambler's *Background to Danger* and Deighton's *The Ipcress File*, that the talker is not there primarily for purposes of information or delay. The Lecturer Beside the Screen is signaling, "Watch this fellow. He may be danger!" This one also is a good illustration of the fact that, in the mystery, there are likely to be no "free" motifs.

The Lull Before the Storm is much like the Fool to Worry signal, but it is treated more objectively. During that quiet week-end in *Jaws*, with no shark and no trouble, the reader knows the writer is setting the stage for action. This one was also planted early by Poe. Remember how, at the beginning of "The Purloined Letter," the narrator and Dupin are enjoying "the twofold luxury of meditation and a meerchaum" when the door is thrown open to admit M.G.＿＿＿, the Prefect of Police, with his singular problem? (293-4)

Step by Painful Step can be used chiefly for purposes of delay, but there is danger in prolongation so extended that it may lose the reader's interest, as was sometimes the case with the "silly-ass" eccentric detective who prattled and procrastinated until he effectively ruined the story. The device has its best impact as a signal at the primitive level, as in the encounter story where the protagonist literally advances painfully step by step to accomplish a rescue, like the one in the closing pages of *The Tower*

As a result of conditioning and conventionalization, these signals are prime representations of the process of cultural shaping and reader readiness discussed in Chapter 2. The promise implied in conventions like the Solitary Figure and the Exact Time is practically automatic with most people from non-reading experience, and so in all probability is the Lull Before the Storm. The Fool to Worry signal is freely used in non-formula fiction, and so is the change in pace and point of view. At the same time, it is hard to account for the danger-signal in the Dinner Party convention or the alert in Excessive Detail without previous experience of these signals in the formula story.

We are ready to turn now to the idea of the promissory plant, which is basic to the Suspense Process. These plants may be either messages or signals that the author sows along the way in the narrative, and they are "promissory" because the reader is assured that something will come of them. A good illustration is the unpredicted change of mode in Jack Higgins' *Luciano's Luck,* in the Death Card episode. This is a story strongly dependent upon realistic elements, set against the background of real history (the allied invasion of Sicily) and real characters (Lucky Luciano and Dwight Eisenhower), with the result that the intrusion of a supernatural element late in the book has a jarring effect. Just before the big climatic conflict, a Sicilian woman is telling fortunes with Tarot cards. Savage, one of the commando group, turns up the Death Card, which the woman quickly hides, making him think it is the Three of Cups (Happiness) (240-1). With the plant in place, the Suspense Process takes precedence over reality; an accurate Tarot prediction is inappropriate in this setting, but the reader reacts to the stimulus and would be disappointed if something did not come of that Death Card. So, for the next eighteen pages he is kept in suspense watching Savage. When Savage is indeed killed the following day we are satisfied; our author has observed the convention and kept his promise.

Some of these promises are planted for the reader to remember and some for him to forget, at least temporarily. Higgins's Death Card is an example of the former category, and so is the cigarette case in Knebel and Bailey's *Seven Days in May*. In that story Paul Girard, the President's agent, leaves Gibraltar with all the summarized evidence of the conspiracy concealed in a cigarette case. All he needs to do is to fly this information back to Washington and the government is saved (170). The reader is not likely to forget that cigarette case, especially when the plane crashes and burns, killing Girard; just in case he does, however, he is reminded a few pages later with the description of the pitifully few objects recovered from the wreckage, including "a crumpled cigarette case, its silver cover jammed in" (209). The plant-to-remember need not be a physical object, of course. It may be an ironic remark, like Whitman's good-bye to the shark-hunters in *Jaws*, as they set out on their fateful journey: "I kind of envy you your trip. It should be exciting" (222).

The plant-to-forget-awhile is often more effective than the first type because of the impact created by something that has been lying just below the surface of recall suddenly emerging to full conscious recognition. This is a favorite device of the mystery: as the narrator of *Rear Window* thinks about that window he has been watching, he is aware that something about it had disturbed him (25); the disturbing element is left lying for ten pages, whereupon it appears as the solution of the whole puzzle. The same is true of the harmless-sounding reference to "our only crime" (25) early in *Miss Pym Disposes*, disregarded by the reader as school-girl talk, but surfacing in the resolution as a real condemnation.

Plants, as we have pointed out earlier, frequently become clues in the mystery, but they can serve the purpose of "straight" plants just as easily. For examples we can turn to the novels of Lillian

O'Donnell, who has considerable expertise in the handling of both. The whole structure of the mystery-detection of *Ladykiller* is built on an elaborate promissory plant: an account of the early criminal career of Frank Salgo closes with the sentence, "Then he met Nancy Hurlock" (15), and the point of view turns completely away to apparently unrelated matters. When Nancy is murdered and Frank turns up as a suspect, the reader keeps trying to fill in the pieces and is finally completely misled into the false assumption that the promissory plant is a *clue*, which of course in this case it is not. In the next novel, *Casual Affairs*, O'Donnell performs the reverse trick, converting a promissory plant into a clue. Early in the story (58) we are admitted to the information that Lucine Northcott, an interior designer, redid the Isserman apartment, one of those casual pieces of knowledge that adorn most mysteries. It is not until toward the end that we catch on to the fact that this was an important clue: Lucine therefore would have a key to the apartment.

In the encounter-type story especially, promissory plants frequently have a cumulative effect, even to the extent that they determine the structure of the narrative right up to the point at which the reader has a full understanding of all the factors converging on the resolution. It would require an almost superhuman resolve for the reader of Hailey's *Airport* to put the book down at that point at which the wounded plane is finally approaching touchdown, knowing as he does that there is a stuck plane still blocking the runway, a demonstration of angry residents inside the terminal, a love quadrangle to be resolved, and an impending suicide(425). Almost any hack can develop cheap sensation through the use of menace, but the tension Hailey develops is the result of those messages and signals planted from the beginning of the narrative, that add up to a powerful drive.

We should also note another use especially characteristic of the tale of encounter, the pre-emptive promissory plant, a device an author may use to prepare his reader for a disastrous or partially disastrous conclusion. Although the formula never promises completely happy endings, many readers will be disappointed if things turn out too badly. The writer, who feels some obligation to preserve plausibility by allowing only partial success, can play fair with his reader by planting a suggestion that a part of the struggle may be lost. Some of the people trapped by the fire in *The Tower* are not rescued, but

Stern has already pre-empted the possibility by having one of the rescuers remark, "If we get anybody out of there alive, it's going to be a bloody miracle" (207). In the detective mystery, the formula itself is pre-emptive: we will not tolerate a mystery that goes unsolved, but we must always be prepared for the perpetrator's escaping detection or arrest.

The purpose of messages and signals is to draw the reader into the story by supplying him with knowledge that will make him care what happens next. Here, of course, we apply two of those "basics" stated in Chapter 1: Suspense takes place only when the reader is involved in the story, and suspense is dependent to a far greater degree upon what the reader has been told than upon what he wants to find out. We recall Daiches's caution that suspense is "not dependent on ignorance of the eventual outcome but on waiting for the inevitable to happen,"[4] and Eco's illustration of the Harlem Globetrotters versus the home team. In her early book on mystery-writing Carolyn Wells calls attention to the importance of the principle of intimation in the development of suspense. Speaking of *The Woman in White* Wells says, "The secret of Collins' power lies not in mere description but in suggestion. He excites us not by what he tells us but by what he does not tell us."[5] Here is where we must be cautious: subtlety and indirection are effective only to the degree that the writer makes us aware that there is something he is not telling us, which is the real nature of suggestion. The principle that it is the ghost we don't see that scares us works only if we know there *is* a ghost. Mere restraint and economy are not enough in the popular formula story.

The position of the knowledgeable reader naturally involves a strong sense of superiority and ego-gratification. *The Andromeda Strain* is a work that bristles with esoteric scientific jargon of such awesome nature that the lay reader may feel intimidated. Michael Crichton, though, carefully admits the reader to a few elements unknown to the scientists, thus giving him the opportunity to chortle smugly and whisper, "You don't know the half of it!" Bram Stoker achieves the same kind of effect in *Dracula*. After the first section, the participants are still very much in the state of mystification, but the knowing reader has moved on to the level of anticipation and suspicion. In a well-managed story, the most trivial fact or the most innocent observation is thrown into bold primacy by the prior knowledge of the reader.

One other evidence of the influence of reader-knowledge is its ability to affect our values and allegiances. In Forsyth's *The Day of the Jackal* we find ourselves pulling for the would-be assassin, because we know him, have watched him prepare, step by painstaking step, for the murder of Charles de Gaulle. Not so in Knebel and Bailey's *Seven Days in May*, where General Scott is seeking to oust the President; we know the President, but the general is the outsider. How many American readers found themselves cheering for Arkady Renko in the last section of Martin Cruz Smith's *Gorky Park*, while Renko is in conflict with the F.B.I.? How many law-abiding mystery readers of a couple of generations ago were drawn into loyalty to Raffles and Nick Carter, as a result of the same process?

There is one kind of plant to which we want to give particular attention because, effectively used, it constitutes an especially powerful hook. We will call it a *conditional* plant, because it does not so much promise later developments as it suggests the circumstances of the author's agreement with the reader. Its strength lies in its ability to create tension between two opposite stimuli, the forward thrust of privileged knowledge and the backward pull of retrospection. Daphne du Maurier makes effective use of the device in *Rebecca*: by the end of Chapter II we have all the basic information about the destinies of the narrator, her husband, the other chief characters, and Manderley. From that point forward, the reader experiences an extra measure of tension when he meets Mrs. Danvers and Favell, knowing that they will have both disappeared by the end of the story, and when he comes upon the scene at Manderley, knowing that beautiful place will soon be in ruins. The effects are simultaneously those of foreshadowing and retrospection. "To appreciate a mystery," says E.M. Forster, "part of the mind must be left behind, brooding, while the other part goes marching on."[6]

The effect can be accomplished in several ways. Du Maurier's handling of it in *Rebecca* is *predictive* foreshadowing, in the sense that she suggests all the chief events in the story except, of course, the solution of the central mystery. Lillian O'Donnell in *Casual Affairs* uses a *narrative* approach, developing a mystery plot up to a point, including a suggestion of a crime and a possible suspect, whereupon she abandons the story completely for something apparently unrelated. Both of these approaches are fairly handy, partly because of their potential for a bell-ringer effect: when we meet Mrs. Danvers and the others in *Rebecca* we have at least heard most of their names and when, in the O'Donnell novel, we suddenly come upon a tie-in between the new plot and the apparently abandoned one, an alarm should go off back in our memory.

The other two methods of conditional foreshadowing are somewhat less obvious and more dependent on suggestion than on substance. The Preface to Robert Ludlum's *The Bourne Identity* is composed of two short news stories dealing with conspiracy, international diplomacy, and assassination. This plant, which represents *dramatic* foreshadowing, leaves the reader with almost no facts but with a strong sense of impending crisis. When we examine the hooks Ludlum uses in this novel, at the end of the present chapter, we will see how these dramatic hints support the major mystery. The other type is one almost never used in popular formula fiction, the *allusive* element, typified by the Flitcraft story in Hammett's *The Maltese Falcon*, which will also receive more detailed attention later.

We do not want to miss the irritant effect of each of these uses of foreshadowing/retrospect, which could be simply annoying in another type of novel. Ordinarily, we do not like to have a plot started and then dropped, but the very context of the formula story exerts two kinds of control that keep us from simply slamming the book shut (or switching channels). First, we know that, in this context, nothing can be regarded as unimportant, whether a half-developed plot or a couple of newspaper clippings; and second, everything will fit into place before the story ends.

At several points we have taken note of a habit of writers of calling attention to the author's own participation by making the reader ask, "Why is he doing this?" Whenever a writer pointedly and repeatedly returns to some apparently minor character, or admits the reader to some piece of privileged information the question of Who? or What? becomes less important than Why? When the reader finds himself raising this question habitually, that is, when he tends to watch the process instead of being merely carried along by the story, he is participating as a privileged insider, an objective participant who has reached the level of genuine appreciation. This is a quality so often evident in those contributors to the Letters columns of *The Armchair Detective* and *The Mystery Fancier*, people who have moved from the status of fans to the level of sharers in the author's creative experience.

The position of privileged insider is naturally indigenous in the idea of formula. The formula conditions the reader to the extent that he becomes accustomed to listening for his author's messages and signals. The very fact that this is a mystery or an encounter story promotes the activity. It is, moreover, an operational experience, almost completely unrelated to content. The reader finds his perceptions working independently of the story, the process of focus, for example, becoming more important than the actuality of the Solitary Figure or the Exact Time.

This function is a reciprocal experience, shared by author and reader. The reader, for his part, tends to watch the writer more closely than in other stories, and the writer, in return, tends to feed the reader more information and direction. The relationship between an experienced, sensitive writer and a reader who has attained the level of privileged insider is much like that between master and pupil who have been together a long time. Suppose, by way of analogy, that I am a doctoral candidate working as teaching assistant under my senior professor, who is my personal friend as well as my mentor, and under whom I have had considerable coursework. I sit in the back of the room auditing his lecture in an introductory course. While he instructs his freshmen, he is also communicating with me on an entirely different level. He rolls his eyes ceilingward as he breezes through an in-joke shared by him and me, but levels a hard glare my way when he comes to that point on which he tripped me up in seminar. While the novices take conscientious notes, I am telling myself, Here it comes or Watch this now. To return to the figure of the veteran reader as privileged insider, this major professor is the Lecturer Beside the Screen; what the freshmen are hearing is the Voice of the Novel, while I listen also to the Voice of Cognition.

We can illustrate the level of appreciation of the privileged insider in several ways. He anticipates the recurrence of a familiar situation, recognizing, for example, that there is no such thing as a simple "disappearance" in a mystery: the chances are that murder has occurred. He catches the point of a piece of irony or an in-joke. He re-lives an experience in which he had guessed wrong in an earlier book and refuses to let a writer mislead him once more into jumping at a hasty conclusion. His enjoyment is probably no greater than that of a first-time reader, but he has gained the position of partner in the creative process.

Since we are discussing popular fiction, we need always to bear in mind that the purpose of all these devices is to get the reader interested and keep him that way, make him care what happens next, keep him turning pages. "First and foremost," says Richard Martin Stern, "the reader must care...The reader must care, and that means he must have an interest in the characters. Plot alone will not do it..."[7] Another author, Desmond Bagley, contributes a useful and accurate designation, the"hook." Discussing the ability to grab and hold the reader's attention, Bagley writes,

I characterize this as the *hook*. On that first page a character must do or say something, or the opening situation must be such that the reader is compelled to ask himself, "What happens next?" You have planted a hook...There must always be at least one—and preferably more—hooks to catch the reader's Attention.[8]

We will conclude this discussion of the dynamics of suspense with an illustration of the skillful use of a number of devices as hooks in Chapter 1 of *The Bourne Identity*, by Robert Ludlum. Ludlum writes the novel of the giant conspiracy against civilization, which characteristically opens as a mystery and develops into an encounter-type story. Ludlum's books habitually go to the top of the best-seller lists immediately upon publication, a dependable sign of a previous history of successes. Chapter 1 of *The Bourne Identity* is almost a showcase example of how to hook a reader and keep him hooked.

The Preface to Chapter 1 is the strategy we cited a few pages back as an example of the "dramatic" type of conditional plant. The story opens with the presentation of two apparently related but irrelevant news stories, the first from *The New York Times* of Friday, July 11, 1975, dateline Paris, and the second an Associated Press dispatch from London, dated Monday, July 7, 1975. Both stories are written in a sensationalized news style, full of allusions to the legendary assassin Carlos, crime and affluence. One plant in the second story especially will shortly produce a bell-ringer in the mind of the reader. The assassin is described (from un-named sources) as "good looking, courteous, well educated, wealthy and fashionably dressed," a sure hint to be on the lookout for him. This article concludes with a dispatch from Caracas that the assassin was using the name Ilich, and a clencher from the local informant, "He told reporters he did not know where Ilich was now." With that the subject is dropped, and the scene shifts at the beginning of Chapter 1 to the Mediterranean.

Note how much Ludlum has done, in two pages, to prepare his reader for the suspense buildup. Specifically, we know we will watch for a Solitary Figure, probably Carlos, more probably Ilich, who must surely be a Russian agent. We are primed by a number of other plants, offering questions but no answers, hints of "guns and girls, grenades and good suits, a fat billfold, airline tickets to romantic places," and the like. Our knowledge at this point is based almost entirely on suggestion and intimation but—if we have been previously conditioned by the formula—the Voice of Cognition reminds us that everything is likely to be important. The very act of abrupt abandonment and switch of point of view is itself a clear signal that something big is coming. Thus, we begin Chapter 1 with our attention "marching ahead and looking back" as a result of some deft foreshadowing.

We are on board a trawler plunging through the stormy Mediterranean, there are gunshots, and a solitary man, obviously wounded, falls into the sea. The sense of danger is intensified at once, when the man hears an explosion rip the trawler apart and tells himself that he has won (14). Here the allusion produced by the conditional plant should begin to control our reading: Who is this? Carlos? Ilich? When he is rescued by a fishing boat, the process goes to work in earnest, as the fisherman watch the eyes of the unconscious man change color from gray to blue. Wounded and half-drowned, the man (now called only "he," but we are to learn later that his name is Bourne) regains consciousness at the home of an aged alcoholic doctor. Bourne has been unconscious for almost four weeks, during which time the doctor has made some discoveries, each of which as revealed is bound to set off echoes in the awareness of the reader: "...Far more than bullets had invaded the man's body. [message] And mind." [signal] (18) Now we discover that Bourne is suffering from complete amnesia, an important revelation that will limit and discipline the rest of the story. Immediately the echoes resume. Dr. Washbourne tells Bourne that in his coma he spoke three different languages; that his appearance has been surgically altered; that his eyes have been affected by prolonged use of contact lenses, despite the fact that his vision is normal; and finally the big one: a tiny microfilm implanted under Bourne's skin, with the name of a Swiss bank and a series of numbers (24). The chapter concludes with Dr. Washbourne's bombshell, "With it you can open a vault in Zurich" (25).

During the course of these revelations, Ludlum exhibits his skill in two ways. He makes Dr. Washbourne a potential menace to Bourne by suggesting that the doctor may be dangerous partly because of alcoholic ineptitude and partly because of greed. With even longer-range effect, he converts a manifest echo into a real strand of suspense. When we learn that Bourne speaks three languages, the pull of retrospect immediately raises a question: Is one of them Russian? Is this Ilich? No. One is English, one French, and one "some goddamned twangy thing I presume is Oriental" (20). The power of the plant holds, but with a new and more compelling direction.

The effectiveness of this chapter in hooking the reader is further confirmation of the principle that suspense is dependent to a greater degree upon what the reader has been told than upon what he wants to find out. The premise holds especially when the supplied knowledge has been delivered via suggestion rather than outright statement. What we know—or can guess—about the wounded amnesiac Bourne has come through successive revelations and identifications like physical characteristics and knowledge of languages, all of them incomplete perceptions, partially answering one question but raising even bigger ones. The experienced reader recognizes that even his guesses about who and what Bourne is can rest on nothing less tentative than those two news stories in the Preface, but he also knows that in the formula story there are no completely free motifs: there must be some kind of connection between Bourne and those newspaper articles.

Even though the suggestions are conditional, Ludlum makes sure we do not miss the point. Three specific plants in the Preface are reinforced in Chapter 1. First, there is the implication of Carlos (or Ilich) and terrorism, naturally echoed in the shooting at sea and the revelations of Bourne's physical appearance. Then there is the international element, conditionally confirmed in his knowledge of languages. Finally, the hint of involvement of vast amounts of money is corroborated by the numbered Swiss account. The strategy is elegant: the foreshadowing/retrospection element supplies the impulse, the cumulative plants hold the apparatus, and the anomaly contributes the challenge. The game thus set up, the author provides discipline and control by imposing the limitation of amnesia on the protagonist. The reader who could put down *The Bourne Identity* at the end of Chapter 1 is the person who can stop after one grain of buttered popcorn.

In Chapters 2 and 3 we have undertaken a summary of the functions of the reader and the author in the Suspense Process. We will turn next to the remaining component, the text of the story itself.

Chapter 4
The Suspense Structure

It will be the purpose of this chapter to show how the Suspense Process determines structure, in terms of phases or states of narration, relational components, and methods of development. We have defined process as the dynamic relationship between the reader and the text. Especially because the term is used in so many different senses, we must first state a definition of structure.

In Chapter 2 we undertook to expand the idea of structure beyond that of simple framework, to include the arrangements of parts within the whole, the relationships of parts to the whole, and the relationships between individual parts themselves. Quite often, definitions of structure are complicated by necessity of distinguishing structure from content, subject matter, or theme. Wellek and Warren avoid the difficulty in this definition:

... "Structure" is a concept including both content and form, so far as they are organized for aesthetic purposes. The work of art is, then, considered as a whole system of signs, or structure of signs, serving a specific aesthetic purpose.[1]

As we have seen, the Suspense Process can be recognized in several kinds of popular formula fiction. There is also a Suspense Structure, which is shaped by process. Purpose tends to determine form in all literature, and, because of their tendency to conventionality, especially in the mystery, and spy story, the ghostly tale, and the encounter story. This is the reason why, as we pointed out earlier, it is impossible to develop a critical theory of mystery-detection apart from the design of other formula fiction. Such an approach naturally leads into questions of classification, of genres and sub-genres. The problem can become a horrendous one if these classifications are made solely on the basis of content or theme. Anyone preparing to teach a course in detective fiction who asks the librarian to prepare a list of all the detective short stories in the college library and receives one that contains science fiction, espionage fiction, and even westerns, soon discovers how many things can be lumped into a classification based on content. The librarian, by the way, may have justification for his choices. How, for example, would you list the stories of Louis L'Amour in the collection *The Hills of Homicide,* which are generic westerns but are also tales of crime and detection?

It will be our purpose, in the following pages, to do two things. First, we will look at some of the conventional structural definitions of three of the popular genres or sub-genres, the formal-problem detective story, the hard-boiled tale of detection, and the "thriller" or "suspense story." After developing some vocabulary, we will see how Process Criticism would generate definitions of the structures of the encounter story, the mystery, the detective story, and the ghost story.

We will begin with the classic formal-problem story, the one most people think of as *the* detective story. The conventional structure of this genre, which was defined by Poe in the Dupin stories, is based on seven standard steps: Problem, First Analysis, Complication, Period of Confusion, Dawning Light, Solution, and Explanation. Although the sequence has been used in thousands of stories, it is still the favorite approach to detection, largely because of its flexibility, which renders it subject to almost infinite variation[2]

As we will see in the discussion of *The Maltese Faction* the classic structure adapts itself to the so-called "hard-boiled" private eye story, but there is another one, introduced by Raymond Chandler and given sharper definition by Ross Macdonald, that fits the tale of the private investigator even better. In Chandler's first novel, *The Big Sleep,* Philip Marlowe is commissioned by General Sternwood to resolve a blackmail plot directed at the General's daughter Carmen. During that first interview, Marlowe learns of the disappearance of a son-in-law, Rusty Regan, and finds his curiosity whetted by that one. The blackmail problem is solved relatively early, but Marlowe can not abandon the Regan disappearance, even when he has been discharged by General Sternwood and has no further formal connection with the case. This plan is what is called the "residual mystery" structure because the solution of one problem leaves a residue of mystery that carries the suspense on into the development of a new plot. The whole direction can become extremely complex, as solutions of existing problems spawn new ones, and main and subordinate plots multiply; at one point in *The Big Sleep* Marlowe is working on five related but separate mysteries. Even so, the residual-mystery structure offers an especially appropriate arena for staging the lone knight errant theme of the heroic private detective.

The third conventional structure is what we have been calling the *encounter* story, the one usually listed by book stores in the"suspense" or "thriller," category. This is basically the simplest structure, built on the situational opposition of Menace(s) and Victim(s). When a distinction is made between "suspense" fiction and the "thriller," "suspense" usually refers to the conflict situation of a frightened-wife-alone-at-night variety, and the "thriller" to the world-on-the-brink-of-destruction type. One point on which most writers of the genre agree is that the essential ingredient is *menace*, Bill Pronzini going so far as to say, "Without *menace*, of course, there is no suspense."[3]

These are three examples of the traditional formal genres or sub-genres of popular formula fiction; we could also mention science fiction, the adventure story, the western, the spy story, and the tale of the occult and supernatural. The thing we must bear in mind is that these groupings are essentially conveniences for purpose of classification. As we have pointed out, the difficulty with formal genres is that some items refuse to stay put, like *The Bourne Identity*, which begins as a mystery and later moves into the encounter type.

Since we are discussing suspense as process instead of literary type, it is not difficult to state definitions of genres in terms of function. Actually, it is the process that determines structure, with the result that the structure of each of the several types of formula story is an adaptation of a basic Suspense Structure.

We will consider the Suspense Structure in terms of four phases or states: cumulation (the phase that accommodates the development of promises, clues, questions, tensions which will determine later effects); postponement (the phase in which the promise of early resolution is deferred); alternation (the period of doubt, where the chances regarding the outcome are uncertain); and potentiality (the crisis, in which chances appear to be favoring a given outcome.) It should be noted that we are not calling these four *steps* in the development of the story, because they are not necessarily sequential. The cycle of postponement-alternation-potentiality may be, frequently is, repeated once or more. The four phases need not be sharply defined; they may (usually do) overlap each other. As a rule they are not of comparable consequence; one whole phase (postponement, for example, or alternation) may be omitted to fit the special needs of the narrative.

In cumulation we customarily become acquainted with the chief relational components of the story. There are, first, whoever or whatever causes the story to move along and whoever or whatever is affected by this movement. To provide a convenient vocabulary we will call the mover (the offense) "A" and the object (the defense) "B." Remember that "A" may be *menace* (the great white shark) or *hero* (Sherlock Holmes), and "B" may be *victim* (the Amity swimmers) or *villain* (the concealed criminal). "A" and "B" may be "sympathetic" or "unsympathetic" (or neutral) in so far as the reader's loyalties are involved; "A" makes the story happen, "B" is its target.

The dynamics of suspense are generated chiefly by tensions involved in the confrontation between "A" and "B"; they are the conditions that make the reader care, in Rodell's words, what happens next. They take many forms (anxiety, curiosity, shock), but their effectiveness in the Suspense Process is measured by the degree to which they get the reader involved in the story. For consistency in nomenclature we will refer to these tensions collectively as "C." As in the case of "A and "B", the nature and intensity of "C" are most easily recognized in the story with an encounter theme. Quite often, though (here again the mystery and the ghostly tale come to mind), "C" will develop before "A" emerges. Du Maurier's *Rebecca* provides an illustration, with a very palpable set of tensions before we are sure who or what the menace is, or whether there is a menace.

Now: our writer places "A" and "B" in the field and lets them produce "C." Immediately he has a problem: if either of his contenders is exceptionally able, what is to keep the story from coming to a conclusion in twenty-five pages? This is the problem of mysteries that feature a super-detective as "A"; if he is as good as his reputation, why should he need 250 pages to clear matters up? The same principle applies to the "B" component: unless he is a complete slob (and, consequently, not attractive as a story element), he should be able to come up with some kind of counter-attack to handle "A" reasonably soon. A good suspense writer will provide a governor, a discipline, to forestall such problems. In Benchley's *Jaws* it even has a name:

the Amity Understanding. A skeptical reader, with a low level of acceptance, could well raise a question early in *Jaws:* Why didn't they just close the beaches and let the shark go away? In which case, of course, there would be no story, so Benchley builds in the Amity Understanding, a compact of silence in the resort town, to forestall panic in such cases and thereby protect the tourist trade. There is a beautiful example in a classic not considered a formula story, Henry James's celebrated ghost story, *The Turn of the Screw.* Fairly early in that tale it becomes evident that the Governess is confronted by a situation beyond her power to cope, at which point the natural, sensible thing would be for her to write to her employer back in London and ask him to run down to Bly and have a look at the state of things. James, of course, was too good a constructionist to allow even the possibility, forestalling it early on with the promise of the young Governess never to bother her employer with any problem whatsoever. This discipline, the exclusion of alternatives (which we will label "D"), takes many directions, but it is almost always built into the structure of an effective story. In Knebel's *The Night of Camp David* it is the power of the presidency that precludes an easy solution to the handling of an insane president. In Stern's *The Tower,* the electrical system in the skyscraper is sabotaged, making easy rescue impossible. Note that in all of these cases the "D" component is not dependent on either "A" or "B" as agent: the electrical failure is independent of the fire in *The Tower,* as the Amity Understanding in *Jaws* is independent of the people who want to close the beach. One more observation must be made in regard to "D": it is the suspense component most affected by social-cultural change. The near impossibility of removing a president was considerably more acceptable in pre-Watergate 1965 than it would be today. In a sense, the writing of a suspenseful story has become more difficult during the past century because of changing mores. Wilkie Collins could place all kinds of obstacles to justice in *The Woman in White,* because of the status of women in mid-nineteenth century Britain. "Good breeding" and tact once supplied a nice set of limits on the choices of people in novels; today, the discipline must be more palpable, like the Amity Understanding.

Cumulation is complete at that point at which the reader finds release from tension postponed. Now the etymology of *suspense* emerges, as our involvement in the outcome is literally "hung under" and "dangled between." At this point, too, the formulaic axiom becomes operative, the assurance that there will be a resolution. Even when the paradox seems to be a contradiction of universal law (as in Tey's *The Franchise Affair*) or a literal point of no return (Hailey's *Airport*), the reader can look at those pages representing the remaining four-fifths of the story knowing he has a contract with his author that promises resolution.

We are already in the phase of postponement or deferral. With what looked like a logical quick solution obviously out of the question, the reader should now be saying, This is more complicated that I thought: no way now to keep the bomber off the plane (*Airport*), no practical way to recover the letter ("The Purloined Letter"). Postponement is the phase in which progress first meets complication, as it does when the menace, thought to be successfully evaded, now looms in full vigor, or the most likely suspect becomes the next murder victim.

In the postponement phase the "D" factor, the discipline, is finally confirmed. This is the point at which the Governess makes it clear that any attempt to make contact with her employer will result in her immediate departure from Bly, and when, in Woolrich's *Rear Window*, the reader begins to understand something he may have suspected, that the narrator is suffering some kind of physical handicap that severely limits his activities and consequently prevents his taking direct action.

We are calling the next phase alternation because it is characterized by a succession of partial successes and near-failures, and tensions are created by keeping the odds up in the air. Instead of a postponed outcome we now have a pattern of progress-complication-progress (or organization-disorganization-organization). This is that stretch of narrative in which a skillful writer can make his book impossible to put down; Woolrich produces a Tantalus effect in "Three O'Clock" by introducing and then removing one hope after another for the man bound and gagged with a time-bomb ticking almost at his feet. This is the phase of the classic detective story in which Nero Wolfe becomes even more insufferable than usual, Ellery Queen becomes almost paranoid, and Philo Vance declares the case hopeless and returns to his translation of Menander.

The reader, of course, is aware of that contract which promises that there will be a resolution, but now a new tension can be generated as he begins to ask, Is it possible that, just this once, the hero may be defeated, the mystery unsolved? As John Cawelti points out, one of the strengths of Alfred Hitchcock was his ability to hold the viewer dangling for just a moment over the possibility that, this one time, he might depart from the conventions of the formulaic suspense film.[4]

The uncertainty must not be overly prolonged, or a writer can lose us through pure vexation. At this point he may suggest, Hold on, this one may be winnable after all. This is potentiality, the stage in the classic mystery when the great detective becomes taciturn and enigmatic, when Wolfe calls in his private operatives and refuses to tell Archie Goodwin (and, hence, the reader) what is going on.

Once again we will draw upon non-formula fiction for the prototype of a figure that frequently enters the story here. About midway through William Faulkner's *The Bear,* when Old Ben has defied all the hunters' efforts to kill him, Boon Hogganbeck finds a great brute of a dog and says, "He's the dog that's going to stop Old Ben...His name is Lion." The Lion Figure is a familiar convention of the formula. He is the do-or-die effort about two-thirds or three-fourths of the way through the story and is chiefly successful but at a price: Old Ben is killed, but Lion dies as a result. He is most easily recognized as a person, like Quint, the fishing boat captain in *Jaws.* Quint appears at the predicted point, shows an almost psychotic hatred for the shark, finally achieves its death, but at the price of his own life. The Lion Figure may be an object, like the crucial cigarette case in Knebel and Bailey's *Seven Days in May:* the case is recovered, but its owner, Girard, is killed. It may be a plan, like the attempt to grab the bomb in *Airport:* the plane is saved, but the bomb explodes, killing one person. Thus, the Lion Figure is a special case of peripeteia, representing a turn in favor of the "sympathetic" side and achieving victory at a sacrifice. It is a signal as well as a structural element. The reader senses the impending turn of affairs as soon as the Lion appears, especially when he is introduced with such drama as at the conclusion of Part One of Forsyth's *The Day of the Jackal.* The Commisaire announces, "The best detective in France, messieurs, is my own deputy, Commisaire Claude Lebel." "Summon him," says the Minister of the Interior (174). The reader with a feel for formula must react, Here it is.

Potentiality is the helter-skelter stage that, if the writer has succeeded in generating real suspense, will rush along toward resolution, holding the hooked reader through all kinds of temporary frustrations and tedious explanations. A skillful mystery writer like Michael Gilbert can even use the breakneck tempo of the potentiality phase to hurry the reader right past one or two important clues *(The Black Seraphim)* and make him want to kick himself for missing them (a palpable form, incidentally, of reader involvement). The prevalence of formula can be used to advantage in this final phase, as Clancy demonstrates in *The Hunt for Red October*. We reach the point at which the Soviet submarine has been safely appropriated and the participants are engaged in prolonged self-congratulation, but the perceptive reader knows better than to join in the letdown, not with eighty pages yet to go, and especially with one hostile sub still unaccounted for. The experienced reader gets much the same kind of satisfaction here as a veteran baseball fan who watches things being set up for a double play; an experienced writer knows how to set things up in such a way that the reader is sure to notice his preparations. The very act of catching on is participation.

What I have attempted to show is that, in popular formula fiction, structure is shaped more by purpose than by conventional genre. In the mystery, the spy story, the ghost story, the head-on encounter story, the purpose is to maintain suspense, to keep the reader turning pages. The writer may have any number of private purposes, (advancing an ideology, satirizing a fault), but the inherent purpose of popular fiction is to absorb the reader, to make him want to buy the next book in the series, and—most especially—to tell his friends about it. These are the conditions from which sales figures spring.

Thus in the cumulative phase the writer must get our attention despite competition. He does this, structurally, by creating an interruption in the order of things: the man in uniform appears at the door of the world-renowned physicist with the singular message,"There's been an accident"; the police investigate the murder of a victim everybody (or maybe nobody) hatred; the Head of Section lays the green file on his desk and taps it meaningfully. We settle ourselves with the assurance that this looks good. When we move into the postponement, our writer's task is to hold our interest without frustrating us: this is not just a brutal murder but something unique in the annals of crime; those nocturnal rappings may be not just something spooky but Something Unspeakable. During the alternation our writer must achieve that balance between the rising and falling expectations which will keep his readers genuinely hooked: the agent escapes the K.G.B. but is speedily re-captured; the missing brother is found, but he is left-handed. At last in the phase of potentiality our author must lead us to feel that just maybe this one could be won. Now the nature of serialization adds momentum to the process, as on the Saturday afternoons of sixty years ago we learned to watch that range of hills just beyond the menacing Indians, waiting for the U.S. Cavalry, or tonight we note that change of camera-angle to the closed door behind the endangered detective right after the 8:45 commercial. In all of these phases, structure is determined by the over-riding process, which is in all cases the same; only the conventions of genre differ.

Not only that: the process itself is structural. Process, as well as substance conveys meaning, with the result that process may become conventionalized. One structural pattern easily recognized in all kinds of formula fiction is the element so briefly introduced that it almost escapes notice, then after an interval re-introduced, re-inforced, and very pointedly dropped, and after a much longer period brought back upon the scene as a major plot factor. Notice how often this conventionalized process appears in the analyses that follow: Van Dine uses it with the Greene library in *The Greene Murder Case*, Gilbert with the poisoned coffee in *The Black Seraphim,* Clancy with the suspicious cook in *The Hunt for Red October,* and Macdonald with the Silent Listener theme in *The Chill.* As suspense strategy the device is superbly effective, but it works equally well in the mystery and the encounter story, and it makes no difference whether the subject is a character, a sensation, or a theme. The meaning is carried by the conventionalized, structured process.

Besides narrative phases and relational components we need to consider the Suspense Structure in terms of methods of development.

In the discussion of Josephine Tey's techniques for developing suspense in Chapter 2, we characterized the technique in *Miss Pym Disposes* (the building up of mystery through sequences of hints, suggestions, and paradox) as rolling a snowball, and that in *The Franchise Affair* (the problem-solving approach) as peeling an onion. In most formula stories, especially the mystery, and most particularly in the detective story, the writer characteristically rolls the snowball for a while, then converts it to an onion and peels it. *Miss Pym* is a model of the type of mystery development favored by Ngaio Marsh, the protracted accumulation of mystery until very late in the novel, followed by a swift analysis and resolution. *Franchise*, which gets to work on analysis very quickly, is after the model of the Sherlock Holmes and Philo Vance type of detection. Sometimes a writer can squeeze an extra drop of suspense by moving the story along without revealing whether he is rolling a snowball or peeling an onion, as in the example from *The Ipcress File* in Chapter 3.

The most familiar line of development in the suspenseful formula story is the simple one, progress-complication-obstacle-progress: the fire seems to be under control, the communications system does not work, the elevators are out of operation, an alternate plan is developed to rescue the trapped victims. Convention has reinforced the "C" of this formula, as the Voice of Cognition reminds the reader that when things are going badly we can still look forward to some kind of resolution, but when they are going well we can watch for signals of bad times to come. The tale of the supernatural, however, customarily develops along a somewhat different line, organization-disorientation-disorganization-re-organization. We begin with a rational world in which problems can be solved by science or the church. When the unsettling manifestations begin we turn to the psychiatrist or the priest for help. Disorientation comes about when the victims discover that neither establishment offers any support, as in *Dracula* and *The Exorcist*. Disorientation gives way to complete irrationality (disorganization), and stability begins to return only when the victims find a new ground by accepting the plausibility of vampirism and demonology.

Two terms we will be using in the analyses of the several novels, beginning with Chapter 5, also need definition at this point. A "suspense core" is a major sequence of related messages, signals, and structural elements designed to hold the reader. The core is not necessarily the same as a plot. The death of Norah Mulcahaney's husband and her subsequent adjustment to grief in O'Donnell's *Cop Without a Shield* is an absorbing story on its own account, but it does not constitute a plot. Neither does the sex core in *The Maltese Falcon*, which cuts across both the motive core and the Falcon core. As a rule, an erotic complication constitutes an independent core in the formal-problem detective story, often toned down and sentimentalized, like Watson's love for Mary Morstan in *The Sign of Four*. Minor sequences that support a core are "strands" of suspense. In *The Tower*, the core is the growing element of menace and danger. The faulty construction of the building is a strand, as in the mysterious figure who wrecks the communications system.

Before concluding this discussion of structure we need to return to the question of genres and sub-genres of formula fiction, not primarily to examine genre theory but to show how Process Criticism can offer some simpler alternatives to the traditional classifications.

We will approach the subject by taking a second look at the problem we handed the librarian a little earlier. Suppose you have been asked to prepare a list of recommended detective fiction. Would you include Poe's "The Gold Bug"? How about Collin's *The Woman in White* and Trollope's *The Eustace Diamonds*? Hammett's *The Glass Key*? Ambler's *A Coffin for Dimitrios*? Being a conscientious soul, you turn for help to some of the standard works in the field, like Howard Haycraft's *Murder for Pleasure*, Dorothy Sayer's Introduction to *The Omnibus of Crime*, and Julian Symons's *Mortal Consequences*. Here you will find some help in definition, but even more you will see evidence that the genres of literature have nowhere near the tightness of the genera of scientific taxonomies. Haycraft will not admit to the realm of detective fiction anything that does not include an identifiable detective who performs a recognizable act of detection. He flatly turns down *The Woman in White* ("a mystery rather than a detective novel")[5] and "The Gold Bug" (not a detective story because "every shred of evidence on which Legrand's brilliant deductions are based is withheld from the reader until *after* the solution is disclosed") (9). Sayers, less legalistic than Haycraft, makes some helpful distinctions when she speaks of "the literature of pure deduction" as distinct from other types of mystery, including the supernatural, and finally "tales of sheer horror, without any mystery at all.[6] Symons liberalizes the approach even more, suggesting consideration of the genre *crime* fiction instead of detective fiction,[7] which would take care of questionable decisions like *The Eustace Diamonds* and *The Glass Key*. What we have seen in this digression is a reminder that literary genres are not made in heaven, a caution that should not be lost upon critics who take other critics to task for including, or failing to include, this or that work in their studies of some literary class.

It is possible at least to mitigate some of the problems of genre criticism in the formula story by using the process approach, which corresponds in a general way to the patterns of traditional classification but also cuts across their lines when questions of function are involved.

The method of classification we are using is the one Paul Hernadi calls the *pragmatic* orientation. Assuming that "no concept of genre is self evident," Hernadi offers four approaches to genre criticism based upon clarification of the similarities in which the critic is interested. One basis is "the similarity between the mental attitudes of authors" (the expressive orientation), another the "similar effect some works are likely to have on a reader's mind" (the pragmatic), another between "literary works considered as verbal constructs" (structural), and the other "between the imaginative worlds different verbal constructs evoke" (memetic).[8]

We are following the "pragmatic reader-based orientation on the ground of our concern with identification of the author's purpose with respect to his reader, which raises the question upon which our classification must rest: Where is this book trying to go? How does it get there? Such an orientation recognizes the influence of formula in popular fiction, taking into account that convention and cultural pressures are involved in the process of creating the readiness of a reader.

We will look now at four structural patterns as defined by Process Criticism, using the concepts developed earlier in this chapter.

The purpose of the Encounter Story (broadly corresponding to the "thriller" and the "suspense story" of book-trade parlance) is to answer the question, What is going to happen? The relational components "A" and "B" are obvious: no question who or what is the menace, or the victim. "C" is generated by the conflict of "A" vs "B." The "D" component is clearly defined, as are the phases or states: cumulation usually identifies "A" and "B" as the producers of "C," and the Lion figure, if there is one, emerges unambiguously during potentiality. Development is the simple sequence, progress-complication-obstacle, with the snowball becoming an onion at a point easily recognizable to the reader. It is important to notice that none of these elements is definitional, that is, unique to the Encounter. In a real sense, the Encounter is the prototypical structure of which the others are modifications.

The Mystery (the "pure" or non-detectional mystery) differs basically from Encounter in that it seeks to answer the question, What is happening? "A" (the person, problem, menace) is not identified until late; "B" (the identity menaced) emerges somewhat earlier. "C" arises from the disturbance created by loss of security. "D" is the vulnerability/inadequacy of "B." (Note the difference from Encounter, where "A" and "B" are balanced opposites and "C" is the excitement of a well-matched game.) The cumulation phase of Mystery is the definition of the problem, usually an anomaly oriented to the present (What is happening?) rather than the future, as in Encounter. Otherwise, phases tend to blur into each other, as when it is impossible to say whether an extended passage belongs in alternation or potentiality. Several elements of Mystery are definitional, "A," "B," and "C" as described here being unique to this particular structure. Here is one of those cases in which the functional (process) approach may cut across the formal: many stories begin as Mystery (the spy story, the ghostly tale) and convert functionally to Encounter.

We are treating the Detective Story as a separate sub-genre instead of a class of Mystery for several reasons, including the fact that it undertakes to answer a different question: What really did happen? In this story "A" is the detective, the element that makes the story move. He will occasionally fumble, but most of the time he is the offensive force. "B" is the problem, which would include the guilty person(s). Here we must introduce a new component, the guilty society, customarily including the guilty person, which the detective must cleanse.[9] "D" is the paradox ("must be/can't be") and the obscured past, which hold the story in bounds. "C" is the repeated revelation-frustration of the detective's pursuit. Note that "A" and "B" are definitional in the Detective Story: the whole structure is determined by the opposition of detective and problem. The phases of suspense correspond generally to the classic seven steps of detection described earlier, the Problem as cumulation, the First Analysis and Complication as postponement, the Period of Confusion as alternation, and the Dawning Light as potentiality.

The hard-boiled residual mystery story follows this same structure, with two exceptions: the main core of suspense tends to ravel off into separate strands (the residual mysteries), each of which follows the sequential pattern just described, and the purpose of the story frequently changes to encounter as the private eye meets his antagonist.

For purposes of illustration we will treat the Ghost Story as a separate structure, although, as we pointed out earlier, it too often changes classes. The tale of the Supernatural looks for the answer to the question, Is *anything* happening? "A" and "B" are customarily ambiguous, "A" often so until the end, and "B" may not emerge until late in the story. Often there, is ambiguity as to what *is* "A" and who *is* "B". "C" is frequently present before "A" or "B", in the story in which there is a general aura of uneasiness, undefined until the story is well advanced. "D" is the irrationality-uncertainty-perversity-invulnerability of "A". Of the phases of suspense, one deserves special attention. Postponement is the state during which the progress-complication development yields to the recognition of organization-disorientation.

These examples are offered as alternatives or possibly supplements to, not substitutes for, the traditional structure-based genres. All classifications serve the useful purpose of promoting discussion and facilitating teaching, but all are subject to adaptation. At any rate, to avoid unnecessary complications we will continue in this book to use the formal generic designations, considering the detective story a sub-genre of the mystery.

The pragmatic approach to the description of genres does offer certain advantages, one of which is its flexibility. It can sharpen the identity of classes that have become blurred or trite through long custom, like Mystery. The distinctness is accomplished partly in the definition of the relational components via the functions they serve, like "A" in the Detective Story, so that it becomes unnecessary to explain each time whether we are talking about the Detective Story which is the same thing as Mystery, or the Detective Story which is a sub-genre of Mystery, or the "pure" or non-detectional Mystery. The pragmatic approach also offers the advantage of teachability, by providing a reader-centered framework for interpretation, on which other concepts (archetype, sociology, psychology, feminism) can be developed. It can be the means of raising the level of appreciation if a heuristic method is learned, and most important, it can be taught for carry-over into the study of fiction generally. At the very least, it may provide some standards for interpretation, to give point to the bare plot-summaries that weaken so many book reviews.

In the next nine chapters we will undertake analyses of a variety of examples of formula fiction, using the principles of Process Criticism outlined in Chapters 1-4. We will examine a formal-problem tale of detection of the Golden Age, S.S. Van Dine's *The Green Murder Case;* the first classic of the hard-boiled school, Dashiell Hammett's *The Maltese Falcon;* a more recent English mystery with reduced emphasis on detection, *The Black Seraphim*, by Michael Gilbert; a forgettable police story, *Night of the Phoenix*, by Nelson De Mille; a distinguished police procedural, Hillary Waugh's *Last Seen Wearing...*; two popular tales of espionage, John le Carre's *The Spy Who Came in From the Cold* and Ian Fleming's *You Only Live Twice;* a tale of the supernatural, *Ghost Story*, by Peter Straub; a representative encounter story, *The Hunt for Red October* by Tom Clancy; and a private investigator novel, Ross Macdonald's *The Chill*. In these analyses we will undertake a double task, to test the hypotheses of Process Criticism against the actualities of formula fiction, and to show how those principles may be applied in the critical treatment of such works.

Chapter 5
The Single Insistent Voice
The Greene Murder Case

The Greene Murder Case is the exemplary Golden Age classic detective story. It appeared in 1928, the third in the financially successful series by S.S. Van Dine (Willard Huntington Wright) featuring the aristocratic, recondite, eccentric Philo Vance. The story begins in the standard fashion, with Vance invited by his friend District Attorney John F.-X. Markham to come along and have a look into some strange developments at the home of the Greene family, one of New York's wealthy old households. What appears to be a bungled burglary soon develops into a series of murders, all committed in the spooky old mansion, with members of the Greene family as victims. The story embodies most of the conventions instituted by Poe in "The Murders in the Rue Morgue"—the transcendent detective, the slightly stupid narrator, the unimaginative police, the locked room, and the others[1]— plus the Gothic elements of the mysterious house, the deranged family, and the suggestions of madness and perversion. Julian Symons characterizes it as a "grand imaginative folly,"[2] and he and Jon Tuska both discuss the tour de force Van Dine undertakes in the development of the "And Then There Were None" theme, as members of the Greene household are eliminated, one by one.[3]

Part of the tension is developed through this theme, but the real suspense core is the role of Philo Vance as Lecturer Beside the Screen, to continue our analogy of the story with a film which unfolds the narrative on-screen, while the Lecturer is the commentator who passes messages and signals to the viewers, pushing them along to want to find out what happens next. This, of course, is the role of Vance throughout the twelve novels in which he appears. The verbal tone of this core becomes the persistent *leitmotif* of the story, and after its introduction by the narrator (the fictional Van Dine) it is carried almost entirely by Vance, in his constant insistence on the *outré* nature of this case, with such language as "something terrible and unthinkable going on" (90), "gibbering, nightmarish story...black suggestiveness" (255-6), and "It's damnable!...this fiendish affair" (333). The method is direct suggestion, and the reader is never allowed to forget how fiendish and nightmarish it all is. The Voice Beside the Screen is that of the magician, with his stream of highly colored promises, suggestions of perversion, of the unthinkable and unspeakable, so effective that we may overlook the fact that he delivers only a bunny rabbit at the end.

If we consider Vance the off-screen Voice of the Novel, then District Attorney Markham and Homicide Sergeant Heath are the on-screen voices of fact and incident. Markham's interpretive role becomes clear in those several exchanges between him and Vance, especially the one in which they discuss the murder of Chester Greene; Markham is strictly factual and conventionally logical, but it is Vance's comments that point to the suggestion-beyond-fact, thus generating tension by intimating that Vance knows something worth the reader's taking the trouble to find out (103-4). Heath is an even more pointed on-screen foil, because his prosaic interpretations of events provide opportunity for Vance to voice those highly suggestive interpretations. Heath without Vance would not be able to carry the burden of suspense; it is Vance that makes us care. The author obliges us with a nice distinction between their narrative roles when Heath says, "Hell, Mr. Vance! You're trying to make this case something that ain't—well, natural" and Vance responds, "Can you make it anything else, Sergeant?" (234-5)

The dynamic of the detective story is sometimes represented as a compelling puzzle for which the reader must find an answer, and he is consequently swept along by the power of the challenge, with artful hindrances impeding his progress toward the solution. This is not the suspense drive of *The Greene Murder Case* (and probably not of most formal-problem stories). Barthes's "dilatory morphemes" are all here—the snare, equivocation the partial answer, jamming[4]— but the impulse of the story is thrust, not delay. *The Greene Murder Case* bristles with promissory plants (along with the standard clues of detection, as we will see in a moment), but we should note the number of promises that assure follow-up via the formula, as when Chester Greene speaks of "a feeling I've got" (13), or when Vance assures Heath that he need not hang any hopes on finding the murder gun (26), both plants but not clues. The formula mandates that no author would dare make such implied promises without intention of following them up. Then there is the substantial promise of the Secret Room, the Greene library, "Nobody's been in it for twelve years" (32), which is in itself enough to keep our curiosity warming up on the back burner until the promise is reinforced with another suggestion, "The only room that was not gone over [in the police search] was Tobias Greene's library" (160). These are not clues, but when that library is finally opened, the reader is right there, eager to enter.

One adjunct of the Lecturer Beside the Screen, with his handy promises, is the assurances that there are, in a formula story, almost no "free" motifs: every element is likely to be important. Thus when Vance asks a seemingly off-hand question, we know that some importance is attached, which might be a casual one in another kind of story, but not in the tale of detection, where there are seldom any genuine throwaways. Where we really feel the impact of the forward impulse, though, is in that random listing of the facts of the case— ninety-seven of them!—with Vance's challenge, "They need only re-arrangement and interpretation to be perfectly clear" (320-7). The reader's curiosity is almost unbearably piqued, but who would take the time to rearrange and interpret in the face of what the Voice has been assuring us about the "black terrible intrigue"? We are pulled backward and thrust ahead in a remarkably successful manipulation of the dynamics of suspense.

We need now to develop more fully the distinction between the familiar clues of the detective novel (which are usually regarded as part of the intellectual equipment of the genre) and those promissory plants that represent something more atavistic in the story-teller's craft. The conventional clue appears early, in the snow that blankets the environs of the Greene mansion and is soon associated with those enigmatic footprints as specific guides to detection. There are plenty of others, as dictated by the formula: the fact that three people were shot with the same gun, that the poison disappeared immediately after Rex Greene was shot, and more. Then there are the usual concealed clues, clear in retrospect but obscured at the point of first appearance, like Vance's " *By Jove!* ...That's the thing that's been evading me!" (303), which stems from the tradition of Holmes's diving into the bushes to retrieve a "glittering object," not identified, of course, that turns out later to be a vital clue.

These clues, artfully as they may be introduced, and cleverly puzzling as they may be, are not the essentials of the drive that makes a story impossible to put down. Many of the most distinguished defenders of the respectability of the detective novel have argued that the tale of detection is in essence an exercise in logic, whose appeal is almost exclusively "mental." Thus R. Austin Freeman, one of the staunchest apologists of legitimacy, could go so far as to say that the connoisseur's basic criterion for judging a detective story is that it be "an exhibition of mental gymnastics in which he is invited to take part."[5] Other apologists variously cite such figures as the crossword puzzle and the mathematical equation. It remained, however, for the perceptive G.K. Chesterton to see that there was an even more persuasive rationale for the good repute of detective fiction: it is, said Chesterton, "the earliest and only form of popular literature in which is expressed some of the poetry of modern life." A little later in that passage he compares the investigator with "a prince in elfland," crossing the modern city in which "the lights...glow like innumerable goblin eyes."[6] It is this poetic element, not the puzzle factor, that makes a detective story hard to put down. In *The Greene Murder Case*, the drive toward discovery is, first, all that insistence upon the "damnable" and "fiendish" we discussed earlier, and second, a long string of promises planted in the course of the narrative, that intrigue us more than footprints in the snow or the mysterious gun.

We are, for example given an extended and undisguised thrust in the last paragraph of Chapter VII. The case at an impasse, Vance announces his intention to resume his translation of Delacroix's "Journal" while the police pursue the routine work on the shootings in the Greene mansion. Then comes the hook: "But Vance was not destined then to finish this task he had had in mind for so long." The paragraph goes on to announce the new development, with such language as "a second grim and unforgettable tragedy" which lifted the Greene Case "into the realm of the foremost *causes célèbres* of modern times" as a result of "a hidden death-dealing horror [which] stalked through the grim corridors of that fated house." (100) This is not the voice of the geometry master propounding a theorem but of the stage magician exhibiting the empty hat. It is the voice that dares us to put the book down, and it is heard again when the narrator describes the way Vance becomes "unaccountably pensive" after each of his visits to the Greene mansion, and admits himself unable to fathom Vance's motives in all this apparently desultory behavior (168-9). All these things are promises an author knows he must fulfill, promises legitimized by the formula. There are others, not really promissory but more simply plants along the way that suggest things to come: Vance's accusing Markham of shutting his eyes to the facts (93), and especially his question to Markham, "Have the galoshes disappeared?" (243). These are not clues in the detectional sense, but they are strong generators of suspense.

Besides these messages—clues, plants, promises—the suspense is intensified by a few conventional signals, the most obvious being the Exact Time insistently repeated at the head of each chapter. Actually, "Wednesday, December 1; 1 p.m." has little substantive bearing on the story; its influence is occasioned by the response it suggests, Why is this exact date and hour so important? Not so noticeable is the Lull Before the Storm, that perceptible slowing-down and quieting-down of the narrative that is sure to alert a reader to excitement ahead; Van Dine makes only one use of this one, the conclusion of Chapter VII we have already noted, where Vance appears to be withdrawing just before the case takes its biggest dramatic turn. One other signal, Excessive Detail, is strongly contributory to the compelling impulse felt especially in those esoteric and almost interminable footnotes, specifically the long German texts that document Chapter XXVI. No reader is going to take the time to read all that (assuming he could), but their very presence signals the weightiness of what we have been told is one of the most ingenious and nightmarish cases on record.

We began this analysis by pointing out that *The Greene Murder Case* comes close to being a precise summary of the general conception of the formal-problem tale of detection. The claim is reliably supported by Van Dine's use of the operational principles (focus, interruption, intimation, confidentiality) in a manner that is practically definitional of the classic story. Typically, its holding power relies chiefly on intimation, as when Vance, after a series of interviews with members of the Greene household replies to Markham's irritated objections with "I think I've done remarkably well" (50), we have a feeling that the writer is cautioning us to watch more closely for evidence of Vance's achievement. The effect is, as usual, created through the medium of Vance himself (who never surrenders the "A" role during the story) largely by means of hints and suggestions. It is most apparent in that curious conversation between Vance and Sibella Greene, where he is supposedly interviewing her as a witness (and of course possibly as a suspect), but his exaggerated gallantries are a clear hint that he is up to something (62-3). Note that the intimations we are receiving here are carried only as suggestions, and not as real revelation: the strategy of confidentiality, whereby the reader is overtly supplied information not shared with people in the story, is markedly absent from *The Greene Murder Case,* as it customarily is from the classic puzzle type of detection. Focus is used substantially, as in those precise timings at the heads of chapters, and so is interruption, notably the dramatic news of the death of old Mrs. Greene at the end of Chapter XX.

The strength of *The Greene Murder Case* lies in its effective development of tone, centered largely around Vance as the insistent Lecturer Beside the Screen, with the reiterated "nightmarish...damnable...fiendish" from start to finish and supported by that sequence of promises which endow the novel with its "grand imaginative folly," as Symons calls this and the other successful stories in the Vance series. The weakness of the method lies in the fact that it is too insubstantial to support a long series of tales. The magic act is big enough until the bunny rabbit is delivered, but after a half dozen rabbits the series loses its imaginativeness and betrays only its folly.

More specifically, what is represented in *The Greene Murder Case* as the almost occult, unnatural, unthinkable/unspeakable turns out to be the systematic but rather prosaic elimination of the members of the family by the alien, motivated by envy and greed. In retrospect, we see that Heath had the right interpretation, "Hell, Mr. Vance! You're trying to make this case something that ain't—well natural." Vance does indeed make of it something that ain't natural in his function as magician, transforming the Greene mansion into a haunted Gothic castle, where even those long German footnotes become atmospheric signals.

Chapter 6
The Dynamics of Motive
The Maltese Falcon

Ask almost any knowledgeable mystery fan to name the ten greatest stories of crime and detection, and the chances are that Dashiell Hammett's *The Maltese Falcon* will show up on the list. This novel, usually considered a classic of the hard-boiled type, is actually transitional, a blending of non-intellectual detection into a strictly traditional narrative structure; the meandering residual mystery plot was to be introduced some ten years later by Raymond Chandler. Aside from the question of structure, though, the serious critic of crime fiction feels an even more specific challenge in *The Maltese Falcon*, in that curious little Flitcraft story that is tucked into the narrative in such manner as to demand some ingenuity in interpretation.

The reader's interest in the novel is built around three main cores of suspense, under which all the suspense elements in the story are subsumed. The strongest of them, the one maintained throughout, is the problem of Motive: What is Spade up to? And Brigid? And Cairo and Guttman? In the process of grasping and holding the reader's attention, the question of motive considerably overshadows the early murders of Archer and Thursby. The second core, the Falcon, is not introduced until the story is fairly well along, but the third one, the Erotic Core, starts at the beginning and runs throughout, although it too is overshadowed by the question of motive.

The reader's biggest problem of motive is Sam Spade himself; unlike the ethical detectives—Ellery Queen, Hercule Poirot, and the others—Spade never gives us any insight into what he has in mind. His "daemonic" quality, as Robert Edenbaum calls it, is hinted at our first view of him, with his yellow-grey eyes and the "v" motif of his face, so that he looks "rather pleasantly like a blond Satan."(3) To the unsophisticated reader, Spade's motives are as unclear, through most of the story, as are Brigid's, Cairo's, and Guttman's. He is the first and most obvious suspect in the murders, being directly accused by Iva Archer and later by the police. Now it is not unusual for the detective in a story to be a suspect, but Spade's motives in other respects are open to such question that the reader may feel some tension over the possibility. We are never sure of his sense of values, as when he demands Brigid give him all the money she has, or whether he is exploiting her situation for purely sexual reasons, or whether, in his dealings with Guttman, he is serious or lying. Now most of these questions are answered at the end of the novel, but until that time the reader is steadily teased with the question of Sam Spade the mercenary, murderous philanderer versus Sam Spade the agent of justice.

The Motive Core also envelops the intentions of Brigid O'Shaughnessy. She offers Spade her body, but withholds her confidence. She admits that she is a liar and pleads that she is tired of all the duplicity. When she disappears, the reader may experience some anxiety over her safety, but is just as likely to suspect her of some chicanery at this point. Guttman, with his obvious guile and his reiterated "well sir," is the conventional obvious suspect. We distrust Cairo at his first appearance, especially when he pulls a gun, and it is easy enough to suspect Iva Archer, the obviously faithless wife who lusts after Sam Spade and could easily have killed her husband to remove an obstacle to her gratification. In total, this whole complex of uncertain motives, which includes just about everybody in the story, becomes for the reader a much stronger source of suspense than the need to see the murders solved.

The second core, the Falcon, does not enter the story until halfway through, but after it is established it tends to dominate the whole Suspense Process. Hammett first uses the signal of meticulous detail— always a sure way to catch our attention—as Guttman unfolds the history of the statue over a long passage; then the author plants the suggestion of its value and danger when it is delivered to Spade by the dying ship's captain. After watching Spade take such care with the hiding of the statue, we are unable to take our eyes off the dark bird until the conclusion. Then there is the Erotic Core, which runs through the narrative, from the first arrival of the sexy Brigid in Spade's office until Spade forces her to strip in his bathroom, and it is reinforced by the sexy Iva Archer and her obvious desire for Spade. Thus the suspense framework of *The Maltese Falcon* is triangular, but the Motive Core overlaps broadly into the Falcon and Erotic Cores.

Here is a structural difference that may be significant in the development of the hard-boiled mystery. In *The Maltese Falcon* we have three cores of suspense: the whole complex of puzzling and even paradoxical motives, the image of the Falcon, and the sensual persuasiveness of sex—all in contrast with the unity of action in *The Greene Murder Case,* where the single directional core of suspense is the one dominated by Philo Vance.

As we stated at the beginning of this discussion, *The Maltese Falcon* was historically a transitional novel, with elements of both classic and hard-boiled detection. An examination of the handling of suspense reveals traces of both the formal-problem and the encounter/thriller types of development. Its heavy reliance on the strategy of intimation, with almost no reader confidentiality, is of the classic formula. So is the role of the fictional detective as prime mover of the story; the offensive option is consistently with Spade, as it is with Sherlock Holmes and Philo Vance. So also is the employment of the axiomatic plant, an assurance to the reader that the two mysteries—the murders and the Maltese Falcon—are related and will be tied together before the story ends. The footprints of the encounter type story are just as strongly evident. There are almost none of the conventional detective story clues, and then there is the question of motive (detective's as well as suspects'), which becomes as important as the Falcon and the murders, as far as the Suspense Process is concerned. Finally, there is the Erotic Core, traditionally absent from classic detective fiction but practically indigenous in hard-boiled detection.

No discussion of the Suspense Process in *The Maltese Falcon* would be complete without some attention to the Flitcraft episode, that curious little story Spade tells Brigid O'Shaughnessy just when the tensions of the novel are building to a high point, which we discussed in Chapter 3, as the "allusive" class of conditional plant. The remarkable thing about the Flitcraft story is that it is developed in considerable detail and then left floating; it is not a promissory plant, and it provides no clues. It may jar the sensibility of a reader accustomed to the mystery formula, which characteristically fits everything together before the final solution.

The first step in recognizing the function of Flitcraft in the Suspense Process is to note its structure, which is strictly classic mystery. Spade begins the account with a clear statement of the Problem, with suitable detail and striking rhythmic monotony: "He did not keep...His wife and children...He owned his house...," and so on (55). Then comes the First Analysis, with the customary implied solution: Flitcraft had plenty of money at the time of his disappearance. Next comes the Complication, proving that first solution wrong: his affairs were in order, and he had an important deal scheduled for the next day. Now, the paradox is complete, an absolutely insoluble problem: "He went like that," Spade says, "like a fist when you open your hand" (55).

At this point, appropriately, the phone rings and Spade's story is interrupted by the conversation with Cairo. When he returns, he takes the mystery through the remaining classic steps of the Dawning Light (Flitcraft has been seen in another city), the Solution (Spade finds him), and the Explanation (the revelation of the falling beam that narrowly missed Flitcraft and prompted his disappearance).

Robert I Edenbaum, in his often-cited essay "The Poetics of the Private Eye," calls Flitcraft a "parable" whose moral is man's adjustments to the randomness and dangers of life.[1] Steven Marcus, in his essay on Hammett in *The Poetics of Murder,* also sees in Flitcraft the theme of "the ethical irrationality of existence, the ethical unintelligibility of the world," and finally, "the most mysteriously irrational part of it all," the persistence of people in trying to behave rationally and responsibly.[2] Like Edenbaum and Marcus, Peter Wolfe labels Flitcraft a parable, but he emphasizes the effect—or lack of it—of experience in the alteration of human character.[3] Wolfe, it should be noted, considers the Flitcraft story central to an understanding of Hammett's work, as evidenced by the title of his book-length study, *Beams Falling,*

Aside from its statement of a broadly ethical point of view, what purpose does Flitcraft serve? Edenbaum, Marcus, and Wolfe agree upon the nature of the parable as Spade's communication to Brigid of his own personal and professional code. Edenbaum sees the message as a statement of Spade's determination to live by Flitcraft's vision of "meaninglessness and the hard knowingness that follows it." [4] Marcus likewise reads the story as a revelation of the forces "that guide Spade's conduct and supply a structure to his apparently enigmatic behavior."[5]

Wolfe's interpretation is somewhat simpler: Spade is using the Flitcraft episode to warn Brigid that he may have to turn her over to the police.[6]

In addition to these substantive interpretations, Process Criticism reveals a very significant practical function of the Flitcraft story in the generation of suspense. Two features of the parable call the reader's attention to its importance within the framework of *The Maltese Falcon:* one we have already mentioned, the traditional structure of the parable, which is the same as that of the whole novel and which immediately signals us its importance as a mystery within a mystery; the second is the fact that Flitcraft is also a parable of *motive.* This second factor becomes even more important when we remember that, at the point of its telling, the Falcon has not even entered the story, and the suspense in the novel is completely dependent upon the problem of the motives of Spade, Brigid, and Cairo. Just as the reader is dubious of their purposes, he also finds himself asking, What was Flitcraft's motive in changing lives and identities? Hammett makes certain we do not miss the point, by giving us the reactions of three people to Flitcraft's explanation. Spade accepts it and understands Flitcraft's position. Mrs. Flitcraft considers it silly. Brigid O'Shaughnessy, when the story is finished, comments, "How perfectly fascinating," and immediately changes the subject (57).

Besides its function as structural and thematic support, the parable utilizes two other devices for the promotion of suspense, the strategies of focus and interruption. Focus is the technique of isolation and emphasis, reflected in the abundance of detail in the story: we know what kind of cars Flitcraft drove, the number and ages of his children, and his exact financial assets. The principle of interruption—usually a dependable device for catching the attention—lies in the position of the story within the larger structure. It breaks into the developments, thus constituting an irritation and building tension. Hammett even adds to the force of the strategy with an interruption within the interruption, Cairo's phone call.

Once finished, Flitcraft is not mentioned again, directly or indirectly. As we have noted, it offers no clues and does not constitute the conventional plant. What is lodged in the mind of the reader is an impression of a world of random danger, together with a hint of important developments to come. Hammett signals his intention at the beginning of the narrative by placing Brigid in the role of Lecturer Beside the Screen. Her first reaction is in fact a succinct statement of an important principle of the Suspense Process. She is "more surprised by his telling the story than interested in it, her curiosity more engaged with his purpose in telling the story than with the story he told" (55). Quite often a writer can stimulate his reader to ask Why this? or Where does this fit? for the purpose of getting the reader personally involved. By the very way it breaks into the story and by the sharp change in tone it represents, Flitcraft catches our attention regardless of its content.

Structurally, Flitcraft fits an important slot, represented in the classic mystery by the Period of Confusion, that section of the story that follows the Complication, like the one we noted near the end of Chapter VII of *The Greene Murder Case*, where Vance substantially abandons the case. Just before Flitcraft, all the principal questions are in place, including the motives of the main characters and the promise of development of the sexual element. The same kind of treatment is conventional in the encounter story, often represented by a postponement or flashback about a fourth or a third of the way through

One of the basics of Process Criticism is that process communicates. Thus, to consider the Flitcraft story in terms of narrative substance only is to miss part of the point. Actually, the story serves two purposes, as if the author were coming at us on two frequencies simultaneously. As message it is parable, Flitcraft's vision of reality, Spade's code and his attitude toward Brigid O'Shaughnessy. As signal, it catches us with its parallels to the larger narrative, in its structure, its primacy of motive, its strategies of focus and interruption. In this respect it serves the same purpose as the moving camera in the Hitchcock analogy, arousing our curiosity in the same way it aroused Brigid's to the point where we also find ourselves "more engaged with his purpose in telling the story than with the story he told.

Chapter 7
Suspense Considered as One of the Fine Arts
The Black Seraphim

If any evidence is needed of the vitality of the classic English mystery, in the style of Josephine Tey and Ngaio Marsh, it is present in abundance in *The Black Seraphim* (1984), by Michael Gilbert. Indeed, the parallel is so strong between this novel and *Miss Pym Disposes* as to invite detailed comparison.

Dr. James Scotland, the involuntary protagonist of the Gilbert book, goes down to the cathedral close at Melchester to escape the pressures of London life, much as Lucy Pym accepts the invitation to a brief respite at the women's physical fitness college, another setting from which, in the persistent tradition of the classic mystery, the outside world is excluded. Like Miss Pym, Dr. Scotland is drawn into a murder case almost by chance, he because of his expertise in pathology, she because her stabilizing influence has made her indispensable. Both books take their time feeling their way into the main plot; each is well into its second half before a crime is committed, and in each case the suspense leading up to overt investigation must be sustained through other devices than detection-and-search.

Functionally, *The Black Seraphim* should be classed as a mystery that ultimately evolves into a detective story. The snowball is rolled in such leisurely fashion that the reader may be only mildly aware of the building tensions that will assume such prominence when the peeling of the onion begins. Other characteristics of the mystery are present, like the vague designations of "A" and "B," the offensive and defensive roles; the long period of cumulation and the blurred demarcations of the other phases of development; and the absence of the operational principle of confidentiality, which is characteristic of both the mystery and the detective story. *The Black Seraphim*, like *Miss Pym Disposes*, is a novel dominated for most of its length by the question, What is happening? converted to What really did happen?

75

when the murder is under investigation. It should not escape our notice, by the way, that these two novels share the theme of the limits of human understanding. In the Gilbert story it is the bounds of scientific analysis. In the Tey book it is of a more personal nature; Miss Pym tries to play God and fails.

Michael Gilbert has long been a master in the creation of suspense. In *The Black Seraphim* he raises the process to the level of fine art. The artistry becomes evident early, in the handling of a number of strands of suspense that are pulled together to form two dominant strands, which are in turn articulated into the one central core of the story. The magnitude of the task of managing such a structure becomes apparent when we set it beside the single tight core of *The Greene Murder Case* and the three quasi-independent ones of *The Maltese Falcon*. What we will call the clerical strand is produced by the tensions within the cathedral close, generated by the rivalries and antagonisms among the church community. In juxtaposition to this one is the strand of municipal corruption, and the two meet in the town-gown or church-versus-state conflict. The erotic (homosexual) strand is less insistent than the others and really supports the clerical strand.

The foundation of this remarkable structure is laid in Chapter One with an instance of figurative foreshadowing that takes the form of metaphor and serves the function of predictor. Upon Dr. Scotland's arrival at Melchester, the reader finds himself in the middle of what could be a scene from *Alice in Wonderland,* a game of live chess in which the Melchester choir boys are pawns, and their elders, some of whom will figure prominently in the novel, are kings, queens, bishops, knights, and castles. What is happening is the re-enactment of a venerable occasion in the Melchester Close: a piece of sail cloth, painted in sixty-four squares of black and white, is spread out on the lawn of the Theological College; the bishops wear cardboard miters, the castles straw hats, and the kings and queens paper crowns, and the knights carry riding-crops. The metaphor begins to develop early, as the reader senses the artificiality of the scene, which later is reinforced and given special significance in association with the theme of the novel, when the percipient Canon Lister, the only real scholar at Melchester, cautions Dr. Scotland against too heavy reliance on scientific truth. Arriving at The Pavilion of Truth is very well, says the elderly clergyman, until you find it "one of those constructions on a film lot, all front and no back..." (68) The metaphor is deepened, incidentally, by the fact that this same Canon Lister is the winner of the chess match.

Functionally, the chess game has predictive value, because it is an enactment in dumb-show of two of the major strands of suspense. Most obvious is the hostility motif, the contest itself, which anticipates the clerical conflict within the Close, between the elements who support the Dean and those who back the Archdeacon. We should not miss the point that the contest has the basic quality of a game, not a struggle between good and evil. "You mustn't make the mistake of supposing that what we have here is a simple case of the good against the bad," says Canon Lister. "It's a case of two different versions of the good in conflict with each other." (66) The erotic strand is pre-figured in one small episode: Canon Maude, who will later try to kill himself as a way out of his homosexuality, affectionately pats a captured chorister-pawn on the head and murmurs some words of sympathy, which are mildly rebuffed by the boy.

As conditional plant, the metaphor serves the same purpose as the Flitcraft episode in *The Maltese Falcon:* both have a foreshadowing/retrospective function, both cause the reader to keep looking back over his shoulder as the story progresses. Like Flitcraft, the chess episode is not mentioned again, except in Dr. Scotland's dream that night about bishops and castles, and in those distant echoes in his later conversation with Canon Lister. Moreover, as in Flitcraft, the metaphor serves as a vehicle for the Lecturer Beside the Screen, a voice that is never completely silent throughout the story. The similarity holds only in respect to their functions, however. The chess game is no parable, teaches no lesson, and consists of only one static scene, in contrast with the classic framework of Flitcraft.

One evidence of Gilbert's artistry is his ability to keep his reader interested through that long rolling of the snowball, that extended stretch before anything really sensational happens. Here is no initial presentation of a puzzle for the reader to worry along until it is solved. We are up to page 107 before a suspicious death occurs, and it is another thirty-seven pages until confirmation that it was murder. To this point our author has kept us moving along with well-planted promises, some of them obviously demanding answers and some (like the chess metaphor) so carefully woven into the design that we sense rather than perceive them. All of the promissory plants serve to confirm the functional classification of *The Black Seraphim* as a mystery: the "C" element, the tension, is felt long before the emergence of "A" or "B."

Some of the promises anticipate short-range treatment, as when the wife of Henry Brookes asks before the critical chapter meeting, "Will there be a fight?" (53) the reader tenses at the probability that a fight is coming up, otherwise the question would not have been asked. The long-range promise is represented at the beginning, when one of the first things we learn about Dr. James Scotland is that he is an expert in poisons, a clear commitment that poisons are likely to be involved, else the matter would not have been mentioned. Some of the plants lead into genuine questions that must be answered in the story, like the repeated suggestions concerning the Dean's past history, and all of those nagging hints about Canon Maude's problem. Occasionally there are little throwaway plants, like the passing mention of somebody named Gilbourne (102); when that name pops up seventy-five pages later, the reader should ask, Where have I heard of him before?

The aesthetic restraint is most evident, however, in the handling of those plants so introduced as not even to be noticed. When it becomes known that the Archdeacon's death was the result of poisoned coffee, the reader may sense that he has missed something somewhere along the line. He should, because Gilbert has skillfully prepared him for just that reaction. Quite early in the story it was a discussion of the taste of coffee, in a different context; then just a few pages later a mention of Henry Brookes's homemade peach wine, which he re-distilled into brandy, reinforced by another, somewhat further along. So, when the question is raised at the inquest, where the murderer could have obtained distilling equipment, bells should start ringing in the reader's mind. One of the best ways to maintain the Suspense Process is to keep the reader asking questions or, if he is particularly responsive, slapping his brow for not having caught it sooner. In another instance, Gilbert so obviously tags a plant as to make it almost impossible to miss: just before the resolution of the mystery, James Scotland sits gazing around a comfortable drawing room, when his eye lights upon a fine pair of *famille rose* bowls. If the reader is paying attention (as he should be, having been conditioned by the matter of the distilling outfit), he will remember that name from somewhere earlier, especially when he is signalled, a paragraph later, that just at this point James finds his mind "wandering down strange tracks" (183). Actually James had seen two bowls of that same pattern in another living room earlier, and it was the association that started his mind down the strange paths.

There are, of course, the standard clues, as when nicotine poisoning is mentioned during the inquest, putting us on the alert for cigarette smokers. There are also concealed clues, designed to irritate the reader just enough to keep him moving along, as when Dr. Leigh gives Dr. Scotland a summary of findings from the chemical analysis and then says, "I needn't tell you what that means" (193); most readers need very much to be told what it means, and do not want to stop until they find out.

Most especially, Michael Gilbert is an artist in emotional foreshadowing, the stimulation of vivid images in the consciousness of his reader. The process of preparing the reader for coming events by means of strongly colored emotional impressions it sometimes done symbolically, as it is in that scene in which James sits looking at the cathedral late at night, watches its shadow creep toward him, and has an uncomfortable feeling that if he does not get away quickly it will fall on him (45). Gilbert can also handle figurative foreshadowing: at a later point in the story James is in the cathedral listening to the reading of the ninety-first psalm, "Thou shalt not be afraid for any terror by night...nor the sickness that destroyeth in the noonday" (105). Almost immediately the Archdeacon, who has been served coffee during the noon luncheon, is stricken and dies. The ability to stimulate vivid images in place of overt, literal description is best seen in the erotic core, which centers around Canon Maude's tendency to become involved with the choirboys. The sense of the erotic is strong, managed by a fine sense of suggestion. James gets the idea (and so does the reader) when one of the cynical townsmen at the pub recites a poem beginning "His height of desire was a boy in the choir" (25). The tension is heightened a few pages later when we learn that Canon Maude has written a love letter to one of the boys. We are given a hint of its wording, but never the text itself. Michael Gilbert knows what many another writer needs to learn, that the thing that makes sex intriguing in print is its private associations and that a reader can be stimulated into all kinds of sensual imagery by means of suggestion, where he may soon become jaded by repeated literal description.

Another manifestation of the artistry is Gilbert's command of a suitable array of signals, notably the Lull Before the Storm and the Change in Tempo. When, for instance, James and Amanda during their long walk sit for a while atop Helmet Down, look out over the fields of Southern England and comment on the peacefulness of the scene, the reader is alerted to prepare for developments—which do indeed begin to take shape, culminating in murder. Gilbert has always been a master of pacing, and toward the end of the story he employs one of the cleverest tricks with tempo to be found in any of his books. Around page 199, as events are nearing the climax, he works something like the football draw play, racing the tempo so that the reader, hurrying, hurrying to find out whether the police will arrest the Dean, rushes right past one of the final clues, the initials "H.G.B" on 201.

The Black Seraphim is a "cool" novel, its basic artistry originating in its ability to stimulate reader-response by suggesting more than it states. This quality produes the Reader-as-Author effect we discussed in Chapter 2, where the reader feels his perceptions working independently of the text. He finds himself, for example, interpreting the chess figure in terms of the very fact of its presence in the story rather than its significance as metaphor only. In the vocabulary of Process Criticism, it stimulates the Voice of Cognition instead of overwhelming the reader with the Voice of the Novel exclusively, as DeMille does in *Night of the Phoenix* or, less stridently, Van Dine in *The Greene Murder Case*. The effect of the "cool" medium is the one experienced by some listeners in the early days of television, who reported a preference for radio drama because they could imagine more intriguing sets than the TV designers could build.

Chapter 8
The Poetics of a Shocker
Night of the Phoenix

To this point we have analyzed three novels of recognizable merit, one a tale of ratiocinative detection, one a prototype of the hard-boiled private eye school, and one a murder mystery with minimal detection. Now we need to address a question: Is Process Criticism applicable only to well-wrought books? Or, in the case of the formula story, is the Suspense Process identifiable only in such books, and is reliance on the process consequently a guarantee of literary excellence and financial success? The answer of course is no on all counts. The process is evident in just about anything written for the mystery market, the "suspense" market, or the "thriller" market, regardless of merit. Conversely, the presence or absence of a recognizable Suspense Process is not an indicator of quality; the first aim of Process Criticism is interpretation; evaluation is secondary.

For a demonstration of the principle we will examine Nelson De Mille's *Night of the Phoenix*, a scarce-remembered police story, one of three paperbacks published in 1975 and never developed into a series. Nobody would accuse *Night of the Phoenix* of literary merit. Its mode is sadism and what book-club fliers call "explicit language and violence." Sergeant Joe Keller, the protagonist, is almost slavishly cast in the mold of Spillane's Mike Hammer, with the customary paranoia and excessive brutality, and even Mike's tendency to preachiness. The order in which we are considering it, immediately following *The Black Seraphim*, offers an opportunity for contrast. The Gilbert novel achieves much of its appeal by evocation of the Voice of Cognition, whereas *Night of the Phoenix* beats the reader over the head with the Bellow of the Novel. One result of this frenetic approach to narration is that the writer may miss opportunities for effective creation of suspense, as De Mille does when he overlooks a good climactic effect, as we will see shortly.

Night of the Phoenix is a bitter novel, built around the themes of the violent legacy of Vietnam and the deceit and ruthlessness of the C.I.A. Chapter I is an instance of the narrative type of foreshadowing/retrospect promissory plant; the story begins in a steamy, stinking swamp, where the C.I.A.-employed professional killer Morgan is stalking and shooting Viet Cong. A helicopter arrives, presumably to take him out, but instead the C.I.A. messenger informs Morgan that he is to be left in the swamp to die, comparing him to the attack dogs of the K-9 Corps: "They are so mean that they can't be brought back to the States. They're killed here when their handler goes home—" (15). Morgan kills the messenger and goes back into the swamp, leaving the reader with the assurance that here is a dangerous menace who will be back for revenge. At the beginning of Chapter II the scene has shifted to New York, with no sign of Morgan—yet—and the reader is left to wonder at the connection between the swamp episode and the big-city police scene. Characteristically, though, the opening has left two plants that will shortly re-appear, the names of two C.I.A. agents, Engels and Hauptmann, and a repulsive image, the fat, slimy leeches that attach themselves to every warm-blooded surface in the swamp.

The technique, an employment of the"narrative" type of conditional plant, is much like that of *The Bride Wore Black* and *Dracula*. As Sergeant Keller and his cops go about the job of trying to solve two mysterious, unusually brutal murders, in co-operation with the C.I.A., since they are obviously C.I.A.-related, the reader finds himself watching for Morgan, who is sure to be involved. When the names of Engels and Hauptmann enter the story, and especially when the second murder involves a particularly nasty piece of business with leeches, the reader is bound to be drawn into the story with a Here he is now response. De Mille, however, disregards the opportunity he has created, ignoring the empathetic advantage to be gained by making each incursion of the menace more dramatic, more sensational than the one before. The first two of Morgan's (presumed) murders are so hideous that they could hardly be surpassed, with the result that the climactic effect is lost, and the suspense strategy is weakened by the author's having led his high trumps first. The failure to follow up an advantage like that is typical of the quality of *Night of the Phoenix*. The very tone of the story is so abrasive that the sharp outlines necessary to the effective workings of the Suspense Process are tattered.

Most of the stridency is personified in Sergeant Joe Keller, N.Y.P.D., who assumes the "A" role as soon as he enters the scene, in keeping with the structure of the novel of detection. The other relational components are just as clearly defined. The ominous Morgan is "B," with the complication that the police must try to get to him first, to keep the C.I.A. from killing him. The "C" element is the tensions created by this contest, with suitable pursuit, shock, and open combat. The "D" component, the discipline that keeps the story in-bounds, is the secretiveness and obstructionism of the C.I.A., who block Keller at every turn. One structural difference between *Night of the Phoenix* and the traditional detective novel is the amount of knowledge supplied to the reader, which is more characteristic of the encounter story. Most of this reader knowledge, however, has to do with the Morgan development and hence is valuable to both the foreshadowing effect and the double irony of the conclusion.

Development of the Here he is now! effect is accomplished on a long-range basis, from the time we leave Morgan in Vietnam until we discover, at the end, that the killings were purposely disguised to look like Morgan's work. We have no clue to his physical appearance, with the result that he could be just about any of the rugged males in the book. Then, as the story progresses, we are never allowed to forget that Morgan is around. At one point the suggestion is so casually negative as to prompt the knowing reader to recognize its real intent: in a conversation with one of the C.I.A. men Keller "absently" makes a reference to 9-mm ammunition which, as the reader knows from Chapter I, is what Morgan used, and consequently nobody is surprised when, on the next page, the C.I.A. man suggests that Morgan is alive (63-4).

The long-range Morgan theme is supported by several other promissory plants. Some of these are medium-range, like the sinister C.I.A. agent Jorgenson, who is the object of Keller's suspicions for a while, and the two agents, Hauptmann and Engels, mentioned in the Morgan episode in Chapter I, who soon re-appear as the first murder victims. There are several short-range plants that sustain suspense over stretches of a dozen pages or so, like Hauptmann's presumed dying message and Keller's unexplained announcement that he is going to take a vacation, both of which the reader doubts and both of which are shortly resolved. As usual, these plants are more effective sustainers of suspense than are the standard detectional clues.

Night of the Phoenix is a "surface" novel, in the sense that it depends almost entirely upon substance for its effects, with minimal exploitation of the communicative power of process. The result is most clearly evident in the almost complete absence of signals, whose function is mainly subliminal. The one exception is the Solitary Figure at the beginning, where the camera picks out the lone sniper in the Vietnam jungle. De Mille declines one chance to develop the Exact Time as a signal of tension, as he does the opportunity to employ the Lull Before the Storm; most of the lulls are simple delay, with postponement dependent on Keller's obscene eccentricities, plus some minimal police analysis.

The structure of *Night of the Phoenix* is, as we have said, unexceptional for the detective story. After the Vietnam introduction, Morgan surrenders his role as protagonist, and Keller takes over as prime mover until the resolution. The tensions are the normal ones, dependent only in part on the reader's involvement in the Here he is now effect and (especially toward the end, after the Morgan theme has lost its impact) on the gimmicks of pursuit and shock. The effects are partly those of encounter: after the detective becomes the protagonist, the former menace assumes a shadowy role, and by the time his real identity is revealed, the question has become largely irrelevant. There is another element of the encounter-type story, in the satisfying afterglow (in which Keller pounds the nose of his fallen quarry with the butt of his automatic), but the Spillane-level gratification is followed by the surprise ending, more like the detective story.

It is not failure to follow the suspense formula that makes *Night of the Phoenix* an inferior novel; the contours of suspense structure stand out all over. It is rather the author's failure to follow up the advantages offered by mastery of the process, like the opportunities for emotional dividends implied in the Morgan story, and the climatic effect of a series of increasingly hideous murders. It may not be sportsmanlike to match a transitory effort like this one against a masterpiece of suspense like Woolrich's *The Bride Wore Black*, but the plans of the two are so similar that a comparison will serve better than a simple summary. Both novels open with a foreshadowing plant, *Bride* with a brief glimpse of a young woman identified only as "Julie," *Phoenix* with the killer Morgan, both destined to be menaces. After a change of scene without explanation of reason or connection, each novel recounts a series of murders in which the reader's suspicions are increasingly directed toward the mysterious Julie or Morgan. The big difference in level of artistry stems from two conditions. First, Woolrich never lets the reader take his eyes off the main theme: Who is Julie: What is her motive? What is the common factor in these murders? De Mille, as we have seen, clutters the way with distractions, most of them involving Keller and his idiosyncracies. Second, Woolrich endows his four murders with gradually increasing impact, layering them in such a way as to set a pattern, introducing variations as needed, until the reader is ripe to be tricked in the last episode. De Mille uses the same structure but saves his big surprise ending until all the reserve of suspense has been used up.

Chapter 9
The Two Voices
Last Seen Wearing...

It seems to be a special feature of the development of the detective story that the exemplary pieces appear early and remain unsurpassed. This was the case with the classic formal-problem type, for which Poe and Doyle set the standards, and it has been true again in the hard-boiled story, with the works of Hammett and Chandler. It is not surprising, them, that Hillary Waugh's *Last Seen Wearing...*, which appeared in 1952, only seven years after the first police procedural, has never been matched in its class. One quality that undoubtedly confirms the permanent high standing of this novel is its crisp simplicity, which includes its low-key tone and economy of development.

It might be well, then, to begin with an examination of its structure. As I have stated elsewhere, *Last Seen Wearing...* structurally falls into the classic tradition, with the standard seven-step development.[1] Being a detective story and hence relying on the operation of the Suspense Process, it also conforms to the configuration of the four phases of the Suspense Structure, cumulation, postponement, alternation, and potentiality.

Cumulation is that phase of the formula story in which enough questions are raised and enough suggestions offered to convince a reader that here is a book worth spending some time on. This, we are told at the outset, with the lack of emotion characteristic of a police report, is the account of the disappearance of a woman student named Lowell Mitchell from the campus of her college. Only one controlling question is raised during these first thirty pages, Is Lowell really missing? During the perfunctory search of her room by the women officials at the college, her personal diary is discovered, and its most recent entries are examined to find out where she might have gone. By the end of this phase the story material should have aroused

86

the reader's curiosity sufficiently to make him want to know whether Lowell is indeed missing, but even stronger motivation than that is at work. The reader, especially if he has read many stories of this type, will hear the Voice of Cognition: Of course she is missing, and not just "missing"—they never are, especially women. Having had the small sample of a couple of entries, the reader should be asking too, What else is in that diary?

Last Seen Wearing... enters the postponement phase when the police are called in. We begin to get the message when Sergeant Cameron tells Chief Ford, "Frankly, it's a stumper," (31) stimulating the reader to respond, This is more complicated than I thought, the normal cue to the beginning of postponement. Now the controlling question is modified to Where is she? and now the importance of Lowell's diary begins to take shape. Chief Ford starts using it to get information on the missing student's boy friends, and the reader should begin to sense the developing paradox, as one explanation after another is eliminated: not this...or this...or this; then *what*? Again the reader finds his sensibilities especially sharpened if he has had previous experience with the Suspense Process and can maintain his awareness of that axiom of the craft: In the mystery, everything is likely to be important.

As is usual in the detective story, the alternation phase is the shortest in *Last Seen Wearing...* The case begins to look hopeless: "A lot of things were happening, but nothing changed" (92). The police find one lead after another evaporating, and the Lecturer Beside the Screen seems to be cueing us, We just might lose this one. The Voice of Cognition knows that in the detective story they never are lost, but the reader may sense a tingle in the possibility that maybe, just maybe, this one time...He should feel a special hint in the fact that the diary is being kept on the back burner, and, paying attention to the practicalities of writing and reading, he should be telling himself, Something's got to break soon; we're half way through the story.

The discovery of Lowell's hair clip in the river is the first real break since the investigation began, and it marks the beginning of the fourth phase, potentiality. Now the author is saying to his reader, Hang on, we can win this one yet. Soon the basic question becomes, How did Lowell die? and shortly afterward, Who killed her? Now her diary, just as the reader has expected, begins to assume importance as the major source of clues. The first analysis of that diary reveals some indications that were before us back in the opening pages but so adroitly concealed that we walked by them, and they are now interpreted as indicators of probable suicide. Again, the prescient reader will reject the solution, on the advice of the Voice of Cognition, on the ground that it almost never is suicide and also that no mystery is ever solved on page 140 out of 251. His suspicion is strengthened when, late in the game, the police begin to take considerably more interest in one suspect than any of the others had received, a sure giveaway.

The unity of *Last Seen Wearing...* is achieved in a remarkable way, through the medium of definition. The question raised at the beginning of the story is essentially the one answered at the end, modified by changing circumstances from Is Lowell missing? to Who killed her? There are no side issues, no red herrings, no explicit sex or sadism, nor any excursions into other sure-fire attention-getters.

The method of development is one of the simplest in detection-writing: the question is raised, a possible answer is suggested, that answer is eliminated, and so on. Early in the story, when Lowell's disappearance is first discovered, there is a discussion of why she might have left school: Didn't like the other students? No. Been kidnapped? No. Eloped? No. Pregnant? No. Here is one of the advantages of the crime story in the creation of suspense: the right answer (pregnancy) is tucked away among the others and rejected along with them. The only big dramatic announcement in *Last Seen Wearing...* comes when the autopsy shows her to be pregnant, and this shock is saved from bombshell status by the fact that the reader had been told that pregnancy was a possibility.

It is a mistake to assume that suspense in the detective story is created by keeping the reader in the dark. As we have seen, a good mystery writer stimulates the desire to keep reading not by what he withholds but by the information he feeds us in the form of all those promissory plants that characterize a suspenseful story. Sometimes these plants take the form of perceptible clues, as in the remark that Lowell seemed to have something on her mind before her disappearance. There are a number of others, more in the nature of suggestions than clues that make the book hard to put down, especially those that keep pointing to the importance of Lowell's diary, as when the warden, Mrs. Kenyon, first discovers it and remarks, "A diary...Well, well, well" (14), and in Chief Ford's continued interest in it. Most of these plants are intended for the reader to remember: we are told that Lowell "could be dying and not let on" (2), that her sick spell might be an act, and that Ford's motto in such cases is "Cherchez le boy" (32). More remarkable in *Last Seen Wearing...* is the skillful use of plants for the reader to forget temporarily, especially in the use of that diary as a thematic unifying agent. In the early pages we are given an extensive direct quotation from Lowell's account of the past few days, but we do not see any special significance in her eccentric use of exclamation-points after a non-exclamatory sentence or the fact that her apparently casual remarks, "I'm late again" and "Nothing's happened" (16) are illogical in this context. One potent stimulus of reader involvement is to run something like this by him so fast that he fails to catch it, then make him want to kick himself when it is explained later, as Gilbert does in *The Black Seraphim.*

Some of these plants-to-be-forgotten are also cleverly disguised clues. We are not speaking here of the deliberately concealed clue (as when the traditional detective listens to a few words over the phone, remarks, "Aha! Just as I thought" and does not tell the reader about it), but what might be called a camouflaged clue whose outlines tend to be lost against the background of context. An example is Ford's recap of Lowell's activities, in the course of which he says, "She was fine all morning up through her history class. All of a sudden she's back at the dorm feeling sick..." (33). The vital clue, that the change took place in history class, blends into the narrative, as does the remark that "Her history teacher looks like Gregory Peck" (37), also camouflaged in a long string of Lowell's opinions of the older men she knows. Here is one of the advantages of the detective formula in the development of the Suspense Process. A clue need not be concealed and thus suggest a violation of fair play. It can be camouflaged as a common plant for the reader to forget. By the same token, the writer can still play fair by suggesting the correct answer to a question and naturally rejecting it along with a string of incorrect ones.

The fair-play principle affects both sides. The reader is given no privileged information and knows nothing not shared by the characters in the novel. One result of this kind of story-telling is that a novel like *Last Seen Wearing...* almost automatically achieves a high level of acceptance. Its feel of "naturalness" and "realism" actually stems from the careful way in which the reader is made a participant along with some people who seem no more exceptional than himself.

Last Seen Wearing. . .is typical detection also in the relationships of its components. The "A," the mover of the action, appears early (when the police are called in) and plays the role of offense until the end. The "B," the defense, is characteristically felt as a shadow until very late, when he materializes as the guilty party. The "D" effect is produced by that skillfully layered revelation of the secret of Lowell's diary.

The tensions deserve special comment, largely because the method of their creation is typical of the tight, economical over-all structure of *Last Seen Wearing*. . .As a rule they are produced directly by those promissory plants we just discussed. The draining of the lake is a good example: from the moment Chief Ford decides to go ahead, the reader feels a sense of urgency not related to any signal. The stimulation is maintained occasionally by plants like "I saw something!" (67) from one of the policemen. The Peeping Tom incident a little later is another instance, as is the finding of the hair clip. In each of these, the reader is alerted to pay attention; something is about to break.

Last Seen Wearing. . .provides a choice example of the operation of the two voices heard by the reader of a formula story. The effective reader knows that satisfactory participation requires listening to both of these, which should be speaking with approximately equal urgency. The situation in this story, says the Voice of the Novel, is absolute paradox, a denial of reason, something that can't happen but has happened. This voice speaks with venerable authority, from a tradition Poe set in "The Murders in the Rue Morgue" and more especially in "The Purloined Letter," a voice that became urgent in the opening pages of each Philo Vance novel, with its insistence that here is a story unique in the annals of crime, the most baffling case of the century. But the Voice of Cognition speaks in the other ear, There is no such thing as unresolvable paradox in the mystery; read on and see how this writer will work it out. There is absolutely no explanation, says the Voice of the Novel: it is not W or X or Y or Z, and hence beyond solution. There is always an explanation, the Voice of Cognition replies. Go back and take a look at Y, which was treated rather skimpily, or how about V as the real explanation? This case is hopeless, says the Voice of the Novel; for the first time in the annals of crime, here is one that defies solution. The author wouldn't dare, says the Voice of Cognition; no writer who wants to stay in business would leave a case unsolved. Solution! shouts the Voice of the Novel, a completely reasonable solution, and so champagne and afterglow all around! Can't be, the Voice of Cognition answers. It is much too early; something is going to happen. This last one (of which we saw an instance in the suicide-solution in *Last Seen Wearing...*) illustrates the force of conditioning in balanced reading. Anybody who has read Ellery Queen's *The Greek Coffin Mystery*, in which there are three successive solutions, all cleverly worked out and each rejected until the real answer is revealed, knows that a mystery, to paraphrase the Berra Maxim, is never solved until the ending.

The two voices create a special set of tensions that operate independently of those within the story proper. These tensions are like those experienced by the player of a game, especially if he is doing it just for fun. A satisfying game is played under a set of mutually agreeable rules, which provide a sense of order and without which the pleasure of the participation would be lost. Two of these rules, which apply to all kinds of formula fiction, we have called axioms in this discussion, the "bound" motif and the guaranteed resolution. Any writer, then, must find a way out of the paradox or the unexplainable, but must do so without breaking the rules. To stay with our game figure, one of the joys of competition lies in the effort to determine what the opposition is up to, and the reader of one of these novels can enjoy trying to find an answer to Why is he doing this? When Waugh keeps going back to that diary in *Last Seen Wearing...* we suspect that he has something special in mind, in much the same way as readers of Fletcher Knebel's *Night of Camp David* must wonder why that author returns repeatedly to the apparently irrelevant ranch in Texas.

Other pleasurable tensions are aroused by our efforts to recall something from an earlier section of the story, one of those side exercises in which a reader engages quite independently of the development of the narrative itself. This happens near the close of *Last Seen Wearing...*, when the police begin to take an unusual interest in Lowell's history teacher Harlan P. Seward, and the reader starts digging around in his own memory to recover something that sounds familiar about that history class. Often a little smugness accompanies that special tingle, as when the reader knows, as a result of knowledge the author fed him fifty pages ago, that somebody is on the wrong track. This one is absent from a tight mystery like *Last Seen Wearing*...but is a special filip of the so-called "inverted" story.

The low shock level and economy of *Last Seen Wearing*... are not just a demonstration of Hillary Waugh's dexterity. The author repeatedly extends the invitation to his reader to come along, to try his hand at solution, and the result is a maximum level of acceptance. Waugh did not develop *Last Seen Wearing*... into a series, but when he created Chief Fred Fellows, using the same kind of narrative effect, he conceived one of the best-accepted detectives in the history of police fiction.

Chapter 10
Critic, Author, Reader, Spy
The Spy Who Came In From the Cold
and
You Only Live Twice

These two books almost demand comparison. Both belong to the genre usually called "spy stories" or "espionage fiction." Published within a year of each other, they share the theme of the burnt-out secret agent sent on a (presumably) final, crucial assignment. Alec Leamas of *The Spy Who Came In From the Cold* (1963), showing symptoms of occupational fatigue, is permitted one more trip to the Eastern bloc to destroy his old enemy Mundt; James Bond of *You Only Live Twice* (1964), shattered by the death of his beloved Tracy in the preceding story, is sent on assignment to Japan, where he will at last destroy his old enemy Ernst Blofeld. Each story, moreover, has a sex theme. Leamas carries on a love affair with Elizabeth Gold, Bond with Kissy Suzuki.

Classifications by traditional genre, though, are reliable only in a general descriptive sense, as witness the "detective story," which covers everything from The Old Man in the Corner to Mike Hammer. Much more meaningful are those designations based upon the process of artistic creation and the role of the reader as participant. There is, for example, the functional affinity between these two stories in the almost complete absence of privileged reader-knowledge; we are permitted to know only what either Leamas or his adversaries know, and the same is true of the Bond story, with the possible exception of that "obituary" of Bond that shows such strong evidence of formulaic conditioning. Then, there is a functional similarity in the use of the sex theme, in each story, as an independent suspense core.

A basic distinction, for purposes of definition and category, can be seen in the thematic differences between the process elements in *The Spy Who Came In From the Cold* and *You Only Live Twice.* It seems rather obvious that the mode of *The Spy Who Came In From the Cold* is ambiguity, of *You Only Live Twice* the perfectly lucid confrontation of Good and Evil. We are never sure of Leamas's relations with Control and "the Circus," for example; are they attempting to exploit and even destroy him, and does he sometimes hold out on them for his own purposes? The reader is likely to perceive Leamas quite early as an enigma: we are seldom sure when we are following the "real" Leamas and when we are watching the professional dissembler. The relationships between characters might be represented by a double triangle, with the real Leamas at one apex and the dissembler at the other, and the lines of true and false relationships reaching from each apex to the Circus at one extreme and the various Communist agents at the other, and a special line somewhere inside the figure reaching to Liz Gold, Leamas's mistress. The situation in *You Only Live Twice,* in contrast, is one of perfect clarity. There is never any doubt planted in the reader's perceptions that M and the Service are solidly behind Bond, and none that Bond's targets, Ernst Blofeld and Irma Bunt, are the essence of Evil. As far as the reader is concerned, there is no problem of identification and no question of who wears the black hats. As far as formal categories are concerned, both of these are secret agent stories, but in actual process, in the author's aims for his reader, they are radically divergent.

We have earlier mentioned the sex theme, especially the fact that it becomes in each story an independent suspense core. We must also note a crucial difference in the operational uses of the sex core in each. The pathetic relationship of Leamas and Liz Gold is part of the atmosphere for development of the ambiguity and the theme of appearance versus reality. Part of the ambiguity arises from Leamas's talent for deception and part from Liz's membership in the Communist Party. The suspense is generated by repeated suggestions that either or both of them may be putting on an act. The sex core of *You Only Live Twice* serves quite a different function. Frequently it supplies a break in the tempo and thus becomes a device for delay, an excuse for a change of subject without losing the reader's participation. Quite naturally, it serves as a good source of promissory plants, as a new set of geishas is introduced who giggle meaningfully between glances at Bond. The reader is teased, put off, promised in a way that fulfills the analogy of the suspense experience with the sex act.

The main differences between these two stories, however, are not thematic but structural. We have already alluded to one of these, the relative clarity of lines of tension between menace and defender, nebulous in *The Spy Who Came In From the Cold* sharp in *You Only Live Twice*. We should also compare the slow or non-existent emergence of the menace in the le Carre story with the early one in Fleming, plus the absence of any point at which defender becomes attacker in *The Spy Who Came In From the Cold* and the sharp change of direction when Bond counterattacks in *You Only Live Twice*. Most especially, we must not miss the fact that there are two "D" components imposed on Bond (he must carry out his raid without a gun and the true identity of Blofeld must never be revealed), but there are no such restraints in the Leamas story: out-of-bounds markers are unnecessary in a game where the scrimmage lines are not clear.

The reader will feel the structural differences in the amount of help he gets as the two stories move through the phases of the Suspense Structure. There are no sharp breaks in *The Spy Who Came In From The Cold*, with the result that there are extended areas of overlap in which the reader is not sure whether, for example, his author is still developing the problem or is now in the process of complication. Does the cumulation phase end with Leamas's conference with Control (which would be expected) or a dozen pages later, when Leamas seems to be running into trouble on his library job (22, 33)? Now the points of transition are frequently not sharp in the formula story (especially in the mystery), but the obscurity of *The Spy Who Came In From the Cold* is more certainly evident in comparison with the clarity of organization in *You Only Live Twice*, where the reader is told point-blank when a new phase is beginning: "This is nearly the end of my education," says Bond at the end of Chapter 11, signalling the change from postponement to alternation, and in case we miss that, Chapter 12 is titled "Appointment in Samarra." Here the Lecturer Beside the Screen is the high school lit teacher who asks Any Questions? whenever a unit is completed; in *The Spy Who Came In From the Cold* he is the assistant professor in sophomore survey who meets our anxieties and perplexities with blank frigidity.

The situation is much the same with respect to the narrative development of the two novels. Bond makes progress, meets an obstacle, overcomes it, in a progression that makes minimum demands on the reader's concentration. There is even a neat summary (182-3) to keep the reader on track. It is this clear, effortless development that prompts Michael Gilbert to observe that the Bond stories "go down like a drink of iced lager on a hot day."[1] Such simplicity is missing from *The Spy Who Came In From the Cold.* Not only do the obscure motives of Leamas, Liz, and Control make it difficult to recognize an obstacle when it develops, but occasionally the progress-obstacle pattern almost changes into the organization-disorganization model of the supernatural tale, most especially in the treatment of Liz in the second half of the story: Whose side is she on? What is Leamas's attitude toward her? Where is reality?

A good suspense writer wants his readers to ask questions, and where the formula is well defined he wants the reader involved to the extent that he assumes the role of Insider, the observer who feels sufficiently at home with the formula to ask not just What? or Who? but Why? Why is the writer doing this? Where is he taking the story? Fleming obviously depends heavily, for his effects, on his readers' familiarity with formula. We come upon Bond in the opening pages playing the child's game of "Scissors Cut Paper" with "Tiger" Tanaka, head of the Japanese Secret Service. The first game goes to Bond, the second to "Tiger," as is customarily the case in the ingenuous buildup; the reader, familiar with the formulaic axiom that there are no genuine free motifs in the suspense situation, will surely ask, What was *that* all about? Le Carre also prompts us to ask questions, but his technique is not so obvious as Fleming's. He does it by means of repeated hints of intrigue and betrayal, and in suggestions of where he may be leading us. His reliance upon the reader's acquaintance with formula has a negative connotation, suggesting that he may be setting things up for a departure from convention.

The functional difference between the novels can be illustrated by reference to each author's handling of the Solitary Figure, that kind of focus that signals the reader to watch for some special significance in the person or thing presented for his attention. In *You Only Live Twice* the handling is conventional. When Bond in the railway diner with Tanaka feels himself jostled by "a man" who is wearing a mask and who furtively disappears (99), the reader is alerted: Watch this fellow. The subject is reinforced a little later by the figure of "a solitary motor-cyclist" following their car (111) and confirmed beyond doubt when he brushes past Bond in a restaurant (126). Convention demands that this individual become involved in the action, and the reader would be disappointed if he were allowed simply to disappear. He isn't; a little later he re-appears and is eliminated in an entirely satisfying manner (132). Compare his handling with that of Pitt, the man at the Labour Exchange in *The Spy Who Came In From the Cold*. Pitt gets the reader's attention the first time he appears, because Leamas is sure he has seen him before somewhere (29). The reason for our curiosity is confirmed when Leamas asks Control about him and is answered "I know no one of that name. Pitt, did you say?" (51) Pitt then disappears, probably to the disappointment of the formula-conditioned reader. Here is an illustration of the variations in free and bound motifs. In the Bond story there is never any doubt that the jostler is a bound motif; he is an essential causal element. The special twist achieved by le Carre is that he seems to be doing the same thing, suggesting that Pitt is a bound element, but then letting him go free. In the first case we have a component of the transparent framework of a strictly formulaic structure. In the other, the stratagem serves to emphasize the thematic ambiguity of *The Spy Who Came In From the Cold*.

The uses of messages and signals by both writers are otherwise unremarkable, except for that pointed example of the pre-emptive plant in *The Spy Who Came In From the Cold* and the case of reader-preparation, the Bond "obituary," to which we alluded earlier. The pre-emptive plant is the promissory message a writer uses in a story in which he wants to reserve the possibility of ultimate defeat for a "sympathetic" character. In the observance of fair play, and to avoid crude resort to shock, he may insert, early in the story, a plant that will forestall at least some of the disappointment of the reader when his hero is killed. Thus le Carre early in the second chapter has Leamas, on his way back to London, reflect on the way he met failure "as one day he would probably meet death" with cynicism and courage (13). Then, just five pages later, he reinforces the suggestion when Control speaks of "the last of a series of deaths" among their contacts in Germany. Even an attentive reader may not be aware of what has been suggested to him, but he will find himself at least subliminally prepared for the death of Leamas at the end of the book.

The perceptive reader, the one experienced in formula, will not, however fail to appreciate the bald irony of the Bond "obituary" in *You Only Live Twice.* At the end of Chapter 20 Bond lets go the balloon with which he has escaped from Blofeld's castle and drops into the sea. Then, without further development, we face at the beginning of Chapter 21 a solemn *obit* from *The Times,* written by M himself. Now the reader, instead of feeling a chill of apprehension, will be more likely to nod appreciatively at the recognition of an old friend, the Reichenbach Gambit. He knows Fleming is not going to kill off so successful a series character just yet, and besides he has seen Bond come through much worse than this: after all, Kissy Suzuki is down there somewhere looking for him, not the first gorgeous female to rescue Bond from spectacular destruction.

Each of these devices is a manifestation of the Lecturer employed by every writer of suspenseful formula fiction, who prods us along with private signals and messages that are often at variance with the manifest story unfolding before us. His methods are not always the same. He may partly turn his face away when he remarks on the possibility of Leamas's death, as if only to suggest an idea without calling attention to it. While the story on the screen solemnly unreels the Bond *obit,* however, he may simply lift his eyebrows at us as if to ask, Sound familiar?

The frequent references to the reader in the comparison of these two works should remind us that no interpretation of popular fiction can be adequate without taking into account the role of the basic element, the consumer. A popular writer who wants to hold his audience will write with that audience in mind. I doubt if any writers use formal reader surveys in devising their stories, but they most assuredly project an image of the prospective reader. Thus the critic undertaking a reasonable interpretation must begin not with the story but with the writer, seeking to look through his eyes as he in turn views his story through the eyes of the reader.

Especially in the popular formula story, the reader influences the text. The effect is evident in the pervasive obscurity of *The Spy Who Came In From the Cold,* where the ambiguity is not so much that of menace versus victim as reader versus author. The reader is not only uncertain of the motives and attitudes of Leamas, Liz, the Circus, and the Communists; if he is a wary reader, he is probably unsure how he is himself being manipulated. The influence of the reader of *You Only Live Twice* is also evident in the kind of staging designed to give him maximum enjoyment. He is there as a game-watcher, to boo the opposition, cheer good-naturedly for an old friend, and watch for ingenious strategies. His participation in *The Spy Who Came In From the Cold* may take the form of developing and evaluating two scenarios at once: in the trial in East Germany, for example, what is the role of Leamas? Is he there as witness or as defendant? That unreal scene, as a matter of fact, epitomizes the reader's mental activity throughout the novel: Who is friend and who is foe?(166-96) The reader of *You Only Live Twice* is just as much a participant, but he acts more directly under the guidance of the Voice of the Novel, joining with the rest of the crowd in hating Blofeld and Irma, knowing the several purposes of Bond and Kissy, counting the pages until the inevitable victory of the Good People.

We remember also that there is no such thing as the value-free reader; each of us reads as a product of our culture. Here is a crucial issue in understanding the role of formula in the reader's participation in the narrative, which is hardly surprising when we consider that notions of formula, convention, and axiom are themselves cultural concepts. As far as the reader of popular fiction is concerned, formula is the most immediate and most obvious expression of his cultural environment, a point well illustrated in the two novels under consideration: both rely, for reader-participation, on expectations generated by the formula. The difference in the two is that in *The Spy Who Came In From the Cold* the reader is asking whether it is possible that the formula may be violated, whereas in *You Only Live Twice* he gains his satisfaction from the assurance that it will not be. Notice how the author in each case manipulates the formula in terms of his commitment to it. Le Carre keeps his options open with respect to both axioms; we are never sure if there are any free motifs, and we suspect a departure from the conventional conclusion. Fleming surrenders his options; we can be certain that everything is likely to be important, and the only question about the conclusion is not *whether* but *how*.

Chapter 11
Organization-Disorientation-Disorganization
Ghost Story

Peter Straub's *Ghost Story* (1979) was variously described by reviewers in terms pleasing to the ears of the writer of tales of the occult and supernatural, like "horrifying," "terrifying," and plain "scary." It also earned the enviable reputation of Book-You-Just-Can't-Put-Down and, understandably, became a best-seller. *Ghost Story* belongs to a formula which, like the tale of detection and the spy story, seems never to wear out. It apparently profited from the wave of popularity created by William Blatty's blockbuster *The Exorcist*, which was published in 1971 and which offers many points for comparison with *Ghost Story*, as we will see in the following analysis. We will also make reference to two celebrated classics of the genre published some eighty years earlier, Bram Stoker's *Dracula* (1897) and Henry James's *The Turn of the Screw* (1898).

As we noted in the discussion of the two spy stories, identification by means of description of process and structure is often more practical than is classification by conventional genre. That is, we can describe the ghostly tale functionally as a narration characterized by the slow emergence of the menace, including those instances in which it is never finally realized. The same ambiguity may extend to the victim. Both of these circumstances are present in *The Turn of the Screw* and, to a limited degree, in *Ghost Story*. This is also the kind of narrative in which the tensions become evident before the menace and victim have entered the scene, a quality especially well illustrated in the opening section of *Ghost Story*, which has all the earmarks of a case of child-abuse. Here an unidentified man is in the act of kidnapping a small girl and holding her by force during a long automobile trip. The reader is irresistibly drawn into the story, even though he does not quite know what is going on, and it is much later before he begins to catch on to the meaning of those promises

100

already planted in this deceptive passage. With a somewhat different application, the Governess begins to make us aware of some tensions with her "flights and drops" at the beginning of *The Turn of the Screw,* before any of the ghosts have appeared; so, as a matter of fact, does Jonathan Harker early in *Dracula* and Regan's mother in *The Exorcist.*

One other quality is even more distinctly peculiar to the tale of the supernatural. This is a pattern of alternating organization-disorganization instead of progress-obstacle. In the mystery, during the phases of postponement and alternation, the story moves ahead and the tensions are developed by means of a series of partial triumphs and defeats: a question is answered, but another one arises; the detective makes a breakthrough but is confronted by another perplexity, and so on. The same pattern is, as we will see, the mainstay of the tale of encounter, where one victory is followed by a complication or obstruction. The difference is that in the ghostly tale there are, characteristically, narrative stretches of irrationality during which it is impossible to tell whether progress or obstacle is dominant.

Early in both *Ghost Story* and *The Exorcist,* as soon as the menace begins to manifest itself, the prospective victims undertake a defense that is organized on a rational base. In *Ghost Story* it is the Chowder Society, in which they seek mutual support through a form of story-telling therapy designed to allay their mutual fears. In *The Exorcist* the defense is organized around psychiatry and the church. There comes a stage of disorientation, however, in which the victims begin to realize that normal defensive methods are not holding up in the face of growing irrationality. The narrator, Don Wanderley, concludes his first passage in *Ghost Story* by confessing "an unusual feeling" that he will record "at the risk of feeling idiotic," (252) and the psychiatrist in *The Exorcist* at this point first raises the question of demonic possession with Regan's mother (99). The third step in the sequence is disorganization, when the very basis of confidence in a rational world is lost: this is the point at which those seeking a cure for little Regan abandon both psychiatry and the church, and at which Don Wanderley confides to a co-worker, "Nothing is what it seems to be. These creatures can convince you that you are losing your mind."(423)

Now comes the crucial step, which will determine the direction of the rest of the story. At this point the novel must come to terms with experience, deciding whether this is a problem to be solved by logical investigative methods or a case of genuine haunting. The story must, in other words, find a basis for organization. If the theme is irrationality, that new basis will not be logic, as in the mystery, but a contingent frame of reference, a center around which perception can be organized. The story thus becomes rational in a poetic sense, and the reader voluntarily shifts to a new level of acceptance. In *Ghost Story* the organization centers around a recognition that Don Wanderley is willing to accept, that he is himself in an esoteric sense a ghost: "It was the unhappy perception at the center of every ghost story (429). The new core of organization in *The Exorcist* is demonology, to which Regan's defenders turn as the basis for counterattack. The reader of *Dracula* will remember that organization is accomplished repeatedly, as the story comes to terms with the reality of vampirism. In each of these stories, though, it should be noted that it is a rational person who makes the decision to accept and use, without reservation, the rationale of the occult.

Significantly, this never happens in *The Turn of the Screw,* and the refusal of that story to come to terms with the obvious has produced an ambiguity that is itself a work of art. The long-extended controversy over this masterpiece centers finally around two possible readings, the Haunted Children or the Haunted Governess. Now it is important to notice in this connection that the contenders in the debate have racked the text of *The Turn of the Screw* almost to exhaustion and psychoanalyzed Henry James almost beyond recognition, but no one pays attention to that essential, the reader, or to James's intention toward that reader. There are two functional elements to be considered here. One is James's design for this story as represented in the unparalleled artistry of technique. *The Turn of the Screw* is one of those stories in which the buildup of suspense is like the rolling of a snowball, as layer by layer is added until the reader is carried along by curiosity over what is inside. The real genius comes about in the way that the snowball is handled. It can be converted to an onion and peeled, as in most encounter stories and all detective stories. It can be allowed simply to melt, as in a "straight" mystery like *Rebecca.* Or, it can be left to stand on its own as an exquisite snowball, which is the unique aesthetic of *The Turn of the Screw.* The other is the element we mentioned in Chapter 4, the "D" factor, the Governess's Promise, which limits overt interpretation in this case by excluding a major narrative possibility. Nothing is resolved: the Haunted

Children reading holds that the struggle for the souls of the children ends in partial victory. The Haunted Governess interpretation is that, because the outside world is excluded, there is nothing or nobody to pass judgement on the "real" situation, and hence nothing remains except the unreliable word of a psychotic narrator. It would appear that James limited his boundaries in that manner for a reason, to produce an immutable ambiguity.

Mention of narrative development via organization-disorientation-disorganization-organization reminds us that the writer of a ghost story faces a special problem in regard to Level of Acceptance. Obviously, it is not necessary for a reader to believe in ghosts in order to enjoy a tale of the supernatural, but the writer, if he wants to avoid the opposite risks of having his story seem too silly for words or too terrifying for imaginings, must somehow get his projected reader with him sufficiently to persuade him to listen to the lecture while the story unrolls on the screen. Some writers seek to accomplish this end with constant appeals to rationality (especially science), and some by begging the question (as in many "true" stories). Straub's solution is especially sound. He pulls us into the story by making us confidantes, giving us information not shared by any of the others or by almost none. The most noticeable use of reader-knowledge here is the repeated appearance of the ghostly woman who comes on the scene with a changed name but always with the recognizable initials "A.M.," and the sinister man and small boy who enter and re-enter, evoking in the reader a variation of Here they are again. The reader will soon find it easy to accept these spectres because he recognizes them and may even enjoy the irony of their effect on the unsuspecting characters. Stoker gains much the same effect from the recurrent appearances of Dracula. Early in each episode the reader will find himself watching for the Count, anticipating the appearance he will use on that occasion.

Reader-knowledge is produced by means of those promissory plants—messages and signals—to which we have made reference earlier. A reasonably complete discussion of the plants in *Ghost Story* is impossible here, because it would be difficult to find a popular book that makes more abundant or more skillful use of the device. Just one example of the way in which Straub fills his reader's consciousness—and his subconscious—with "hooks," should suffice. A few pages back we referred to that puzzling opening of *Ghost Story*, which has the appearance of a case of child-abuse the abduction of a small girl by an adult male. The technique is the familiar suspenseful one: an apparently tense situation is developed, treated cryptically, and apparently abandoned while the story moves on to other things, an almost certain guarantee of tension as the reader continues to feel the nagging pull of that abandoned story. In this one, the writer takes advantage of the opportunity to plant a number of promises which, if they seem to do little to increase the reader's knowledge, at least sprinkle his mind with hints and suggestions. This is an almost classic example of the conditional plant discussed in Chapter 3. A plot is developed up to a point, then abandoned, leaving the reader to march ahead and look back, wondering what the connection was. The episode makes promises, but they are conditional upon the reader's ability and inclination to recognize them when they are fulfilled. Before finishing that short episode the reader will have heard the names of several people who will appear later as main characters; he will know that the child's name is Angie Maule, the first of that string of "A.M."s later to become signals of evil; he will learn of the man's dead brother David; he will hear the child's perverse answer "I am you" to the man's insistent questions; and he will face the question, at the beginning and again at the end of the passage, *What was the worst thing you've ever done?* All of this is beautifully calculated to pull us into the story, partly because of the natural appeal of an uncompleted sequence, partly because of the suggestions of evil in the plants themselves, and partly because of the bell-ringer effect most people enjoy when a name or a situation pops up later and the reader realizes he has heard that before.

Besides its richness in promissory plants, *Ghost Story* makes skillful employment of a satisfactory number of signals, those stimuli of suspense usually not indigenous in any plot element, that trigger the reader's anticipation. One, the Dinner Party, produces such drama in both this one and *The Exorcist* as to deserve a short review of the principles we discussed in Chapter 3. One reason why a social event tends to be an attention-getter in a hazardous context is that it introduces an element of contrast or interruption, which in turn invokes at least a mild shock. Thus when we read how Chris in *The Exorcist* is planning for a dinner party after just beginning to experience the first disquieting symptoms in her daughter, and how the Barneses in *Ghost Story* have the same plan after a long siege of supernatural manifestations, we naturally begin to expect something: keeping in mind that in a popular formula story everything is likely to be important, we know our writer is essentially promising that something will come of that dinner party and hence the very presence of the event becomes a signal for rising tension. Not only that: the event itself tends to become conventionalized; in both stories the dinner parties follow brief periods of respite from the menace, and both are reinforced by another familiar signal, the Fool-to-Worry convention.

The reader of course is not disappointed in either case. Before Chris's dinner party is over Regan has appeared to her mother's guests as a monster, and the Barneses' teen-age son faints when he is introduced to his dinner-partner, Anna Mostyn, whose spectral manifestation he had seen the night before in an "empty" house (339-40). After this kind of thing happens a few times, a reader will inevitably feel his interest quicken at the mention of a dinner party in a ghost story.

These messages and signals are the essential agents of suspense, because their function is to produce reader-knowledge, without which there is no incentive to involvement. If, as Rodell says, "suspense is the art of making the reader care what happens next," then it seems tolerably obvious that a reader is not going to care much about what he does not know much about; hence, no reader-knowledge, no suspense.

Possibly that is over-simplified, because the definition of suspense really faces in two directions. Daiches speaks in the same spirit when he defines suspense as "an intensification of interest in what happens next," even to wording the objective exactly the same, "what happens next." Another view is that of suspense as the product of stasis, with thrust and delay in a sort of equilibrium. Roland Barthes in the passage we quoted earlier speaks of the "paradoxical" dynamics of a text, created by "the sentences (that) quicken the story's 'unfolding' " and move it along, and the "hermeneutic code" that performs an opposite action by setting up "delays (obstacles, stoppages, deviations) in the flow of the discourse..."[1] Dennis Porter's definition leans more heavily toward the function of delay: "Suspense...occurs whenever a perceived sequence is begun but remains unfinished," and even more pointedly a little later where he speaks of a situation as being "unresolved and therefore suspenseful."[2] We might balk at Porter's "therefore" as implying a little too much causality: no fictional situation is *therefore* suspenseful unless the reader cares about it, and he does not care unless he has been primed by that carefully prepared knowledge his author has permitted him.

The subject is worth discussing here because both *The Exorcist* and *Ghost Story* have reputations as being enormously suspenseful. An examination of the systems of messages and signals will help to explain why. In *Ghost Story* the appearances and re-appearances of the unearthly "A.M." and the frightful man and boy furnish a substantial core for the reader to follow, since almost every one of these produces a shock of recognition that belongs to the reader alone and provides him with an ironic superiority when, for example, Peter Barnes and friend are about to enter an old house and the friend remarks, "I just get the feeling this house is empty" (308); the reader knows it is filled with guilt and ghosts. Who could put the book down without seeing how this comes out? The situation is unresolved, as Porter says, but the condition that makes it suspenseful is the irony produced by the privileged reader.

Delay, then, is not the only determinant in the Suspense Process, or even the main one. The balance of tensions that create the need to read on is really governed by that axiomatic assurance of solution which, win or lose, will be a satisfying one. The delay serves as counterbalance to the thrust, making certain the game is played out to the full sixty minutes, intensifying the gratification of solution. Even the devices for delay become familiar to the point of convention: the gabby eccentric in the detective story who prattles on to distraction, the sudden switch in fictional viewpoint, the profusion of detail, It is the reader's privileged position, though, that generates suspense, not exasperation.

It is puzzling, in a story as well crafted as *Ghost Story,* to meet with a blemish as egregious as the account of the death of little Fenny, which is given to the Chowder Society by Sears James (78-9). As the reader moves through this highly charged scene he may have the feeling of having read these very words somewhere—and indeed he has, if he remembers the death of little Miles in *The Turn of the Screw.* For some reason that is never explained, Straub lapses into James's words, even to whole sentences. Unwilling to let matters rest there, he does it again briefly on page 319: "He held them with the story, speaking into the flames of the candles...," which is a strong enough echo of the opening of *The Turn of the Screw* to attract attention.[3] Obviously this is no place for a suggestion of plagiarism; it is too trivial an instance for that. Neither is the echo an illegitimate device, nor is parody. What troubles us is that in a novel in which every effect is obviously intended toward some explicit purpose, we wonder why an exception without so much as a hint of explanation. A question like this is of special interest to Process Criticism, which sets the purpose of the story as one of its guidelines.

Chapter 12
Modes of Encounter
The Hunt for Red October

The usual scenario for the beginning of a successful career in fiction-writing involves a long series of failures and a trunkful of rejection slips before the aspiring novelist turns out the one success that starts him on the road to acceptance. This was not the case with Tom Clancy, who had published no fiction before *The Hunt for Red October* and had no direct experience with submarines, yet produced in this novel a hit that dominated the best-seller lists for months, and followed up with a string of triumphs. His career reminds us of that of S.S. Van Dine, another newcomer to fiction-writing who started with a sequence of almost unprecedented successes. One thing that unquestionably contributed to the popularity of Van Dine's novels was that, before writing the first one, he saturated himself in the mystery formula and thus entered the market with an exceptional command of the nuances of convention. The effect is clear, especially in Van Dine's early hits, which are almost parodies of the Golden Age tradition. *The Hunt for Red October,* as we will shortly see, fills the same niche as a demonstration model of the novel of the head-on covert international encounter. This combination of conditions should be of special interest to the student of popular fiction: a well-seasoned formula, in the hands of a writer of considerable ingenuity, plus a market for international thrillers comparable to the one for mystery-detection in the 1920's and-30's.

The Hunt for Red October belongs to the type of nations-in-collision, Armageddon-level book written by Robert Ludlum and Ken Follett. Red October is a nuclear-powered Soviet submarine, the most technologically advanced in the world, commanded by Captain Mako Ramius, who decides to defect to the United States, bringing his ship and crew with him. Running deeper, faster, and quieter than any other sub could, Red October strikes out across the Atlantic with the whole Soviet fleet in pursuit. When the Americans catch onto Ramius's plan, they enter the game and try to help him. Thus the stage is set early for a drama in which offense and defense soon change sides, the defense is supported by a second defensive element, and together they assume the offensive role.

This is the kind of story we have been calling a thriller, in which the roles of "A" and "B" are unambiguous, "C" is generated by the contest of "A" vs "B," and the "D" is clearly defined. The alternation phase frequently offers a hint that the contest could be lost by the "sympathetic" side, and potentiality often involves an explicit Lion Effect. Unlike the ghostly tale, the structural phases are distinct, and the narrative development is accomplished by successive progress-complication-obstacle instead of organization-disorientation-disorganization. The snowball is straightforwardly rolled, converted to an onion, and peeled. Actually, since the term "thriller" has been used to refer to such a variety of books, we should use "encounter story" to distinguish it from the mystery, which is the narrative more strongly dependent on questions than on affirmations.

As we noted a little earlier, *The Hunt for Red October* is rich territory for the student of the Suspense Process. The framework of its structure is ten separate promissory plants, each of which produces reader-knowledge that builds expectations and generates tensions. All ten of these skeletal plants are skillfully done, but we will discuss only three of them, one because it is a particularly interesting example of the second type of plant (the one the reader is expected to forget temporarily), and the other two because they are merged in such a way as to constitute something like the double curve of baseball, tempting the reader to strike at a false assumption.

Close to the beginning of the novel there appears briefly a Soviet sub commander named Tupolev, identified as being out on maneuvers at the time of Ramius's defection and also as being a former student of Ramius who would welcome the opportunity to beat his old master in some kind of practice contest. Tupolev remains on the scene for two pages and then is dropped amid a host of fast-breaking early developments and is not mentioned again for more than a hundred pages. The reader, of course, forgets him. His next appearance is for only one page, obviously a reminder that he is around. Now, his image having been reinforced just enough to avoid being lost permanently, Tupolev disappears again for almost three hundred pages. The timing and spacing are ingenious. The real impact of the technique finally makes itself felt at that late point where the U.S. Navy has taken charge of Red October and is easing her into a secret berth. Then, a short paragraph begins, "Tupolev was heading back west" (418), and the promissory plant produces the predictable reaction, What's he doing here? Why him again? This is the stuff of which suspense is made and the kind of thing that makes *The Hunt for Red October* hard to put down. Clancy goes a step further and ties this plant into a familiar formulaic after-effect, as we will see a little later.

The other example, involving the merger of two plants in such a way as to make the reader bite at false bait, is a model case of the power of suggestion. The opening strategy is unobtrusive: Ramius's plan for turning Red October over to the Americans without his crew's knowledge is just going into operation, and in the course of the narrative we read, "The cooks bringing food forward from the galley to the crew were seen to linger in the bow as long as they could" (203), a fairly interesting but hardly sensational statement most readers will forget. A few pages later, though, when two Soviet officials are discussing a secret agent on Red October and one remarks that he is a ship's cook, a bell should ring in the back of some readers' minds. Twenty-five pages later we learn that the Americans have picked up a nearly drowned Soviet sailor about whom they know almost nothing except "He's a cook" (244). At this point even a mildly attentive reader will begin to take notice: Here he is! Observe that the pattern of suggestion is exactly the same as in the Tupolev strand: a short introduction just graphic enough to make an impression but just restrained enough to be dropped from active memory; then a brief flash only strong enough to hold the image in place; and now something rather sharper than a suggestion that the planted element is about to take his place in the scene. Almost any reader, whether experienced in the formula or not, will take for granted that the Americans have found the Soviet agent. Discovery, a little later, that the two are not the same, will produce the effect of a batter who has swung at a curve and missed; he sets his jaw and digs in determined not to do *that* again.

The double curve or draw play is especially effective in the hands of a master of suspense like Cornell Woolrich, who in *The Bride Wore Black* re-introduces his disguised and criminous young woman again and again until we react each time with pleasure, Here she is again! Late in the novel, though, Woolrich runs in an outsider in exactly the same setting, leading us to kick ourselves when we discover we have jumped too quickly. Some of the most popular mystery writers (Agatha Christie and Ellery Queen, for example) were experts at conditioning a reader to accept an entirely false set of circumstances. When this happens, our author, as Lecturer Beside the Screen, has assumed the role of amiable magician who keeps our attention by making us look at the wrong thing. Clancy does not go so far, but he knows how to use the technique.

More effective is his use of the promissory plant to draw the reader into the story by means of privileged information. Sometimes it is only subliminal knowledge, as in the case of our half-awareness that Tupolev has some private design on the plot to deliver Red October to the Americans. Clancy keeps us especially uneasy about Tupolev at that point at which the novel is moving into a stage of afterglow, with U.S. Navy men congratulating Ramius and his colleagues, and vice-versa, on the successful completion of the plot. The reader, though, must decline to participate in the jubilation, for at least two reasons. In the first place, he has that vague uneasiness with regard to Tupolev, especially if he bears in mind that no writer is going to keep a menace around all this time without using him. This is the value of the technique of holding Tupolev half-remembered in the wings: dangers only hinted are more intriguing than those before our eyes. There is, however, another reason for the reader to be alert for more developments. No writer is going to wind up a story with eighty pages yet to go. This is a clear example of the function of literary convention as a contract between writer and reader that allows the reader to participate at a level of higher intensity than if he were only passively listening.

Besides the use of promissory plants instead of questions to keep the reader's interest, *The Hunt for Red October* shows a number of other marks that distinguish the Suspense Process of the encounter story from that of the mystery: the early emergence (and clear identification) of menace and victim, stronger reliance upon signals than we usually find in the mystery, and employment of the Lion Effect and the "D."

From the beginning of *The Hunt for Red October* there is no question of who or what is on the offensive, of what is making the story move. There may be a point at which offense and defense swap sides (as they do in this story when the Soviet Navy gives chase) and one at which two elements unite (as Ramius and the Americans do) to assume the offensive or defensive roles, but no ambiguity of the kind DuMaurier achieves in *Rebecca*, when the story is well advanced before the young Mrs. de Winter knows who is really menacing her.

Signals are those stimuli of suspense that attract the reader's attention not so much by the information they convey as by the very fact of their presence. They are, of course, available to all sorts of writers, but the nature of the encounter story makes them more useful than in the mystery. The most frequent signal in *The Hunt for Red October* is the shifting point of view, which has the effect of catching the reader's interest through the principle of change or contrast. We can hardly miss the point when, just at the moment when Tupolev is about to attack the liberated Red October the point of view shifts five times on a single page (440). The changes themselves do not give us much more information than a single point of view would have; the tension is generated by the very presence and frequency of shifts. The device is not unknown in the mystery, but there it is more functional than suggestive, serving mainly to avoid revelation and to warrant delay.

Two other devices for suspense that are standard in the encounter story serve their purpose in *The Hunt for Red October*, the out-of-bounds marker ("D") and the Lion Effect.

Benchley's *Jaws*, another encounter story, supplies the prototype for the narrative discipline or "D." In the traditional detective story no such device is needed: the density of the paradox insures a long stretch of time before the resolution. In *Jaws*, though, we meet a practical logical problem of prolongation: Why not simply close the beaches and let the shark move away? This kind of question frequently arises in the encounter story, as it does in *The Hunt for Red October*. Why don't the Soviets simply close in on Red October and re-take her before she can cross the Atlantic? Or, that failing, why don't the Americans make contact with Ramius and complete plans for his escape? The answer is that, in the first case, Red October runs too fast, deep, and silent for the Soviets to find her, and in the second,

Ramius maintains strict radio silence. The tension is preserved at a high level without any troublesome questions of motivation.

The model for the Lion Effect is the great dog who brings about the death of Old Ben in Faulkner's *The Bear*. Lion is the last-ditch effort to destroy the menace, which he does at the sacrifice of his own life. Quint, the fisherman who kills the white shark in *Jaws* but is himself killed, is a second example. The Lion Effect in *The Hunt for Red October* is not a living being but a plan, the American plan for getting Red October's crew off her without their knowing the submarine has been seized. It works, but several men lose their lives.

Both of these devices are structural, but both also serve the same function as conventionalized signals in the Suspense Process, because the appearance of either in a story is a stimulus to reader tension. Here is another instance of the fact of the reader as product of cultural shaping and of what we have earlier called formulaic conditioning. As he comes to be more and more thoroughly conditioned to the formula, the reader hears more clearly the Voice of Cognition and develops appreciation at its functional best.

Which leads us into a point that should not be lost: acquaintance with the encounter process is basic to an understanding of the mystery process, if for no other reason than that the bare bones of process stick out more sharply in the encounter story than in the mystery. A little earlier we noted that the "D" component, which features so often in the encounter story, is usually unnecessary in the mystery, because the thickness of the problem serves the purpose of impediment. We were referring to the "pure" (non-detectional) mystery, but the situation may be different in a story that has elements of mystery and encounter, like most of the hard-boiled class. Such was the case, as we noted, with *Night of the Phoenix*, where the secrecy and interference of the C.I.A. served to retard the action. A critic familiar only with the mystery formula might fail in this essential of interpretation.

Another necessity of which the interpreter must not lose sight is that of making careful distinctions between the two. One way of doing this is to define the mystery as a story "based on one or more artfully protracted questions," and the encounter story as one motivated by the reader's knowledge and expectation. Another is to describe the essential differences between them as based in content and theme, and the similarity as the Suspense Process itself. This process is common to all kinds of formula fiction that have suspense as a major intent. Whether it is a detective story, a ghost story, a spy story, hard-boiled or soft-, it shares the Suspense Structure. Regardless of theme or content, the story will be built around the four phases of cumulation-postponement-alternation-potentiality, and it will have elements corresponding to the "A," "B," "C," and "D" components.

Chapter 13
The Tortoise, the River, and the Listener:
The Chill

In an interview in the mid-1970s Ross Macdonald said, "I think that people like a rapid story clearly told, but also with some depth. The mind isn't satisfied...by an account of life that doesn't give the depths of life."[1] In these two sentences Macdonald concisely accounted for his own success as a best-selling mystery writer who has also retained the respect of serious students of the genre. The rapidly moving, clearly told stories gained him an awesome following of committed fans, and the skillful handling of the "depths of life" is attested by the fact that Macdonald's work has been the subject of at least one book-length critical study, two book-length checklists, and an impressive array of essays, papers, and panel discussions.

The ability to manage pace, clarity, and depth is especially evident in *The Chill*, published in 1964. This novel follows the structural pattern of the "residual mystery"; Lew Archer undertakes to locate the missing bride Dolly Kincaid and completes the assignment in just a few hours, but without discovering the reason for her running away or the real nature of her emotional problem. Before any of this can be cleared up, Archer confronts the murder of Helen Haggerty, a woman he has met during the original investigation. As is often the case in a Macdonald story, this new murder, plus the leftover unanswered questions from the disappearance of Dolly Kincaid, carries Archer's search back to two old murders, committed respectively ten and twenty-two years earlier, and into the dark and tangled lives of the Bradshaws, supposed mother and son, who are apparently connected somehow with the other mysteries.

Ross Macdonald achieves a remarkable unity in handling all this complexity through the development of two governing images, one designed for the reader to remember and the other for him to carry along just below the level of recall. The first image is introduced

115

as one of those disingenuous free motifs supposedly intended only to pass some time before the story starts moving again. Waiting in the corridor at Pacific Point College where Dolly is enrolled, Archer overhears a woman student trying to explain the Second Paradox of Zeno to her moderately dense male companion. Achilles, she says, can never catch the tortoise, despite the fact that he can run ten times as fast, because the tortoise has a head start; before Achilles can catch up the tortoise has traveled another distance, and so on: "The space between them was divisible into an infinite number of parts; therefore it would take Achilles an infinite time to traverse it. By that time the tortoise would be somewhere else" (25). Archer overhears this exchange but does not react, because at that moment he sees Dolly coming. The reader of course knows, especially if he is acquainted with the formula, that something will undoubtedly come of this; a mystery writer does not ordinarily spend this much time on a side-issue without purpose.

Nor has he in this instance. Later Archer, viewing the body of the murdered Helen Haggerty, has the impression of time infinitely sub-dividing itself "like Zeno's space" (55), and a little further along he forces himself to think about the paradox: "It was a soothing thought, if you were a tortoise, or maybe even if you were Achilles" (60). Increasingly, as he covers more and more distance and seems no closer to solution, Archer identifies with the Zeno problem, which has now assumed the status of major theme. Tailing two elderly women, one apparently involved in the recent murder and the other in the twenty-two-year-old one, Archer pauses at a paperback stand and picks up a book on ancient Greek philosophy which has a chapter on Zeno. "Archer will never catch the old ladies," he tells himself (161). At this point Macdonald gives the image a new overlay, when Archer reads on to the section on Heraclitus and the analogy of the flow of time to a river. Now the Voice of Cognition should remind the perceptive reader of that fixed law of the formula: Achilles may never catch the tortoise, but Archer will catch the perpetrator. The image shifts its focus, too, as Archer finds time flowing past "like Heraclitus' river" (165).

The Zeno image becomes thematic almost as soon as it is introduced, in the constant reiteration of time-distance relationships. Archer, characteristically, is in almost constant motion, driving from Pacific Point up to Indian Springs to see Dolly's aunt, then flying to Bridgeton, Illinois (Helen Haggerty's home), to get some light on Helen's murder, then back to Pacific Point after a stopover in Reno. The time element is usually expressed in terms of history: Helen tells Archer about an anonymous voice on the telephone, describing it as "the voice of Bridgeton talking out of the past" (35). The time and distance figures assume a kind of congruity as they merge: the "now" image is the murder of Helen Haggerty, here at Pacific Point; the mid-past is the murder of Dolly's mother, Constance McGee, at Indian Springs, seventy miles away and ten years ago; the distant past is the murder of Luke Deloney, at Bridgeton, two-thirds of the way across the continent, twenty-two years ago. The time-distance merger is also symbolically represented in the name of the yacht on which Dolly's father is hiding out, the *Revenant* (the Voice of Cognition should remind the reader of the symbolic name of the dinghy, "Je Reviens," in *Rebecca*), and reinforced by one of Macdonald's celebrated similes when Archer goes down to the harbor to board the *Revenant* and sees white sails "headed shoreward, like homing dreams" (176).

The counter-theme is the Silent Listener, which is introduced and then dropped almost as pointedly as the Zeno image is reiterated. Sitting in the old house at Indian Springs where Dolly's father presumably murdered her mother, Archer is reminded of the framed mottoes on the walls of his grandmother's house, especially the one that read, "He Is the Silent Listener at Every Conversation" (80). No more is said by the author, but the reader can feel the Voice of Cognition at his elbow: Watch this! Macdonald is too efficient simply to leave the motif completely free, and he consequently reinforces it with three hints. Looking out the window from which Dolly was supposed to have seen her father approach the house on the night of the murder, Archer asks how tall she was at the time; shortly afterward he reminds her aunt that Dolly now says she did not see her father; and, as he leaves, he has the impression that the aunt was about to say something more, then changed her mind (81-5). Thus secured, the Silent Listener is tucked away and apparently forgotten for a hundred pages, when Dolly, under sedation, tells the truth about her listening at the upstairs window ten years earlier.

The counterpoise between the Zeno Paradox and the Silent Listener is effective because of the way the two themes are matched. Both call attention to themselves as obviously disguised free motifs. The reader knows there is some special point in the Zeno image because it keeps re-entering Archer's consciousness, literally and figuratively. At the same time, he can hardly escape the tension produced by that business about the Silent Listener, introduced, pointedly reinforced, and then just as pointedly allowed to drop, like Tupolev in *The Hunt for Red October*. The principle of interruption works as effectively with this plant as the principle of focus does with the Zeno figure.

For the most part, the other messages tend to follow the conventional mystery pattern. The promissory plants are both abundant and varied, with a suitable assortment of "regular" plants and clues. Sometimes the Voice of the Novel speaks with an insistence reminiscent of S.S. Van Dine, as when the Dean of Women at Pacific Point tells Archer that Dolly on her wedding night "found out something so dreadful—" (29) and Helen Haggerty tells him a little later that Dolly "has some real trouble—appalling trouble" (33). In general, Macdonald is most effective in maintaining suspense through the use of cumulative plants, whereby many small motivational devices add up to a powerful drive. In terms of mere reality, Archer's decision to fly all the way back to Illinois for a talk with Helen's father is questionably motivated, especially in view of his shaky financial backing at this point. Not so for the reader, however, whose level of acceptance has been adjusted, as a result of plants, hints, clues, and suggestions, to be ready to murder the author if he does not send Archer on that trip.

The narrative framework of *The Chill* is the "residual mystery" structure, which is more suitable to the frenetic, tangled worlds of the private investigator than is the neat puzzle-solution-explanation of the classic formal-problem mystery. The advantage of this type of structure is that it permits the management of a considerable number of related, overlapping lines of inquiry, and it takes its name from the tendency of the narrative to stir up secondary mysteries faster than the original ones can be solved. Typically, *The Chill* opens with the detective accepting a fairly easy commission, the location of the missing Dolly Kincaid, whom he finds relatively early but with the introduction of a strong residue of mystery, the question of the identity of the bearded man who had so upset Dolly, followed soon by a murder obviously connected to the case, then the discovery of the two old murders, and some attendant questions, all finally answered in one big revelation. This is the structure Raymond Chandler developed in *The Big Sleep* and used later in *The Little Sister* and *The Long*

Goodbye. It has also become conventional for the residual mystery structure to bring to light some old, almost forgotten crimes that need solution, and old family secrets and deeply hidden sources of guilt—which has almost become a trademark of the Lew Archer novels.

Ross Macdonald did the American mystery a great service by demonstrating that civilized themes—even those from philosophy—are not incompatible with the purposes of the hard-boiled private investigator story. As this novel shows, suspense is not dependent on violence, menace, and unrelieved pace. *The Chill* confronts the reader with a symmetrical configuration of impossibility of solution (Zeno's Paradox), alternative principle (Heraclitus's River), and assurance of conventional resolution (The Silent Listener) that not only shapes the total structure of the novel but sets up optimum conditions for the functioning of process between reader and text.

Chapter 14
Process and Criticism

Before moving into a summary of the basic ideas in Process Criticism, we will re-state the purpose of this book, as described in the first chapter. Our main concern has been the development of a theoretical base for interpretation of the mystery story, with specific emphasis on the tale of detection. Because the mystery belongs to that type of popular fiction governed by formula, we have spent considerable time on other types of formula stories, especially the "thriller" (encounter story), the spy story, and the ghost story. Actually, it is impossible to gain a full understanding of the mystery without some acquaintance with the general nature of formula.

Familiarity with the encounter structure, for example, is basic to an understanding of the mystery structure, if for no other reason than that the bare bones of process stick out much more sharply than in the mystery. At one point, for instance, we noted that the "D" component, which features so often in the encounter story, is usually unnecessary in the mystery, because the thickness of the problem serves the purpose of impediment. We were referring to the classic detective story, but the situation may be different in a story that has elements of both mystery and encounter, like most of the hard-boiled class. Such was the case with *Night of the Phoenix*, where the secrecy and interference of the C.I.A. served to retard the action. The ability to spot differences and variations of this kind gives a critic the opportunity to speak with considerably enhanced authority as interpreter. Here is another of the advantages of Process Criticism, which recognizes a Suspense Structure common to a variety of popular formula fictions. Regardless of theme or content, regardless of whether it is a detective story, a spy story, a ghost story, or a "thriller," it will be built around the four phases of cumulation-postponement-alternation-potentiality, and it will have elements identifiable as the "A," "B," "C," and "D" components.

Important features of any detective story, for example, can be interpreted on three different levels: the level of the story itself, which is as far as most book reviews go; the level of the sub-genre, the one usually reached by critics with a broad acquaintance with the detective novel; and finally, the level of the whole genre of formula fiction, which lies within the competence of the process critic. Holmes's stratagem for the recovery of the crucial photograph in "A Scandal in Bohemia" will serve as an example. Holmes creates a diversion to gain access to the home of Irene Adler, fakes a fire, and recovers the photograph, but suffers the humiliation of having his disguise penetrated by the very person he sought to outwit. At the story level, the episode can be interpreted as an example of Holmes's ingenuity, which succeeds up to the point where Irene Adler's intelligence proves a match for his own. At the level of sub-genre, it can be placed in the category of the do-or-die stratagem, where the detective hazards everything to break a mystery that will not yield to other tactics. Process Criticism can go a step further, interpreting the incident as an example of the Lion Figure, and placing it in the context of formula fiction and of literature generally.

The theoretical base of Process Criticism rests upon two assumptions regarding the nature of reading. The first is that process (in the case of the popular formula story, suspense) is a dynamic interaction between reader and text. The second is that process itself, apart from narrative substance, conveys meaning; process communicates.

In the opening chapters of this book we saw how recent critical thought has rejected the idea of the passive reader into whose consciousness the book pours its contents. Every reading is an exercise in interpretation; the difference between the eager fan who snuggles up with the latest Dick Francis and the academic critic searching out Freudian implications in "The Purloined Letter" is the difference in the network of expectations each brings to the act of reading. Hans-Georg Gadamer compares the relationship between reader and text to a conversation, [1] and William Stowe, commenting on Gadamer's thesis, supplies another useful term, the act of interpretation as a "transaction with the text."[2] The effect of the story upon the reader is by no means a one-way affair; the reader also affects the story.

Nowhere is this mutuality more evident than in the detective story—an excellent argument, by the way, for the value of detective fiction as an introduction to the study of fiction. David Grossvogel argues that, since a tale of detection lacks a real "hero" (the existence of the detective serving only as a "mere function of the mystery he is solving"), the detective story "invites the reader to participate in [the] unfolding, to play the game actively rather than through the passivity of a demonstration."[3] The veteran reader needs no further proof. How often do we find ourselves turning back to re-examine what looked like a promising clue or cross-checking the accounts of witnesses, in search of error or contradiction? In addition, the very process of narration often produces the effect of drawing the reader into the "transaction," as we will shortly see in a discussion of process as meaning in William Kienzle's *The Rosary Murders*. Then, of course, in the case of the popular formula story, there is the broader influence of reader upon text in the sense that reader reaction determines success or failure; it is the reader, finally, who fixes the direction of formula.

Our other fundamental is that process itself communicates meaning; what things do in a story may be more important than what they are. This being true, a number of implications and conditions must be considered by the process critic in interpreting the popular formula story, because the suspense element is the chief determinant in such stories, and suspense is by definition process. One implication of the communicative function of process is that some episodes and effects in narrative may have no other meaning than as process. Probably the clearest example of the principle is the "pure" signal, like the Dinner Party as Harbinger of Crisis. I more than half suspect that the same logic applies in the case of the Flitcraft "parable" in *The Maltese Falcon,* which seems to be doing considerably more than it is saying. A second concomitant is that the participatory effect of process as communication will vary considerably from one reader to another—hardly an earthshaking insight in itself but serving as a reminder of the place of the Voice of Cognition in suspense: the "process communicates" principle and the Voice of Cognition naturally re-inforce each other. The communicative factor is minimal when only the Voice of the Novel is operative but builds dramatically as the Voice of Cognition develops. In Chapter 2 we drew an analogy between the first reading of a formula story and the re-reading of a mimetic one. We are prepared now to say that reading another formula story is not just an addition to the reader's knowledge but a changed acculturation, a new programming of the Voice of Cognition, an augmented code. The third implication is that in most instances the effect of process as communication is subliminal. Ordinarily we are not aware of the impact of those long detailed lists that seem to have no substantive reference, in those seemingly irrelevant reiterations of the exact time, which are nevertheless building tensions and forcing our participation. Finally, process, like substance, is part of any structure, and it is subject to conventionalization. This last factor is undoubtedly one of the contributory reasons in the capacity of formula for constant renewal, because it adds a whole new exponent to the possibilities for inventiveness, allowing any number of new situations (substance) to be multiplied by the number of ways of handling them (process).

One of the special qualities of Process Criticism is its recognition that tension in a story is created by several means other than the fictional encounter between hero and villain, or menace and victim. It is here that many popular book reviews and even extended articles fail to rise above the ordinary; they are content only to summarize the novel or to draw some generalizations about the conflict and its participants. As we have already seen, one of the best sources of suspense is the contest between author and reader, especially when the author has produced enough stories to establish a considerable following and can depend on a number of readers who relish participation in the game. The contest assumes another form in the conflict between the Voice of the Novel and the Voice of Cognition, which is grounded in one of the oldest and firmest traditions of detective fiction, the friendly contest between "hype" and experience. The other source of tension is the one we have just discussed, the interaction between reader and text. The process critic especially sensitizes himself to this one, seeking to interpret any formula novel primarily in the context of this interaction. He must see evidences of such elements as the employment of promissory plants, messages, signals, and structure in terms of their intended effect upon a projected reader.

I think we can best illustrate the principles of the communicativeness of process, and the interaction between reader and text, and especially the method of the process critic, by an examination of a highly suspenseful tale of detection, *The Rosary Murders,* by William Kienzle. This is a novel in which structure is determined by process and in which the reader is substantially compelled into a "transaction" with the text.

The Rosary Murders follows a familiar plan, the serial murders of eight priests and nuns, with the pathological killer challenging the police to discover the pattern he is following and stop him. The perceptive amateur detective is Father Koessler, who finally breaks the chain and stops the murderer just in time to prevent his carrying out his original design of ten victims.

The story opens with the death of Father Lord, an aged and decrepit priest, in a Catholic hospital in Detroit. His passing is generally attributed to natural causes, but Father Koessler has heard a rumor that death resulted when someone—accidentally or purposely—unplugged Father Lord's life-support system. Before the end of the first chapter we learn that the news-wise city editor of the *Free Press* also senses a possible story in the old priest's death. At this point, though, the most active believer is the perceptive reader, in whom the Voice of Cognition is speaking out strongly: Of course Father Lord was murdered; otherwise, why mention him?

The sense of participation is immediately reinforced by a sudden switch of point of view, when the narrative camera focuses on Ann Vania, a nun teaching a class of second graders. The reader is away ahead of everybody else in the story: this innocent scene is no free motif; popular writers don't focus on something like this without intent. The apparently irrelevant episode lasts for less than one page, but when it is over the reader is assured that Sister Ann will be the killer's next victim, most especially because the last thing said about her is, "Fortunately, she knew of no one who wanted to hurt or kill her" (9), a clear promissory plant. The contract is fulfilled just fourteen pages later, when Sister Ann Vania becomes the second victim.

At this point our author is using one of the fundamentals of suspenseful writing: the best way to draw a reader into the action is to keep him ahead of everybody in the story, by inviting him to carry on his own investigation on the basis of privileged knowledge. The reader begins to sense a pattern, to enjoy an advantage that is reinforced a few pages later with a clear signal. A paragraph ends with Father Koessler's remark, "There'll be another 'rosary murder'," and the next one begins "Father Mike Dailey was having a late breakfast..."(46). The very shock of interruption marks Father Dailey for our attention, and it is no surprise when he is shot dead on page 66.

Notice at this point how many principles of the Suspense Process are at work. Now the Voice of Cognition is especially strong, forcing the reader to watch for the development of a pattern, which he should begin to sense in the alternation of priest-nun-priest victims. The reader, by this time genuinely aware of the tension being generated between himself and the text, should be ready to take a leap ahead of the story, with his own prediction that the next victim will be a nun. The reader is, in short, being programmed, and the process is confirmed when a subsequent chapter begins, "One of Detroit's living legends was Mother Mary Honora" (76).

Once a pattern is established, however, a skillful writer must take care not to lose his reader's participation by allowing predictability to become monotony. Shortly before the fourth murder (Mother Mary, as we suspected), the camera focuses on Father Fred Palmer. This one is a false alarm, and the reader expectedly falls into the trap of anticipating his murder. Not for long, however; when Father Palmer is killed shortly afterward, we already know his death was due to a heart attack, and when the police discover that the rosary in his hand is not one of those planted by the murderer, the reader is already ahead of them. Kienzle also varies his pattern in two other ways. The fifth victim, instead of being singled out by the narrative camera, is introduced as one of three priests, and the sixth, a nun, is introduced while the fifth is still alive.

From here on, the diversity is handled much like the variations on a theme in music; the eighth victim is introduced before the seventh, and the seventh is allowed only three pages in the spotlight, in contrast to the earlier ones, most of whom had twenty or more. The operational principles keep reminding the reader what to watch for, as when those undisguised interruptions break into the pattern with the false alarm and the variations in victims, when the strategy of confidentiality supplies him information not shared by the others in the story, and when those clear intimations of things to come keep signaling his attention. The real transaction between reader and text grows out of the reader's effort to discover the pattern, because the Voice of Cognition tells him there must be one. By the time Father Koessler, under mortal pressure to find the killer's plan and prevent the next murder, begins his analysis of the list of victims (219), the one person looking over his shoulder is the reader.

A good story invites a variety of critical approaches, and in the case of *The Rosary Murders* the temptation is especially strong to interpret it as a social document. A pithy review could easily be developed around the theme of the changing role of authority in the late twentieth century, with special reference to the crisis in Catholicism precipitated by Vatican II. A feminist critic could find an abundance of material for discussion of the changing role of women in the church. *The Rosary Murders,* as a matter of fact, invites comparison with the Rabbi novels of Harry Kemmelman, which have done so much to educate the reading public to the tenets of Judaism. We should find no fault with such interpretations, as long as our critics remember that they are reviewing a detective story, not a handbook on organized religion. As we have pointed out earlier, Process Criticism easily accommodates all kinds of additional interpretation; the critic must recognize first, though, that he is writing about a popular formula story, which is shaped by its own criteria.

To perceive and interpret process, the critic must take as his point of departure the way in which the author is working on his reader. *The Rosary Murders* is especially recommended for study because of Kienzle's ability to involve and manipulate readers of varying levels of experience with formula. The skill is especially evident in the way he keeps us ahead of the story with those patent interruptions and promissory plants that could be missed only by the most neophyte readers. Having done this much, Kienzle performs a small educational service, trapping us with a false alarm but rescuing us quickly enough to restore faith in our own investigative powers. Here is an illustration of the mutual re-inforcement between the Voice of Cognition and the "process communicates" principle: the reader not only asks "Why didn't I think of that?" but says also to himself, "Watch for patterns. This writer may use one to trick me again." The invitation to participation by readers of different experiential backgrounds is evident too in the reader's experience of the structure of the novel. The novice can not avoid sensing it; the very regularity and repetition built into the plot suggests a pattern. The reader becomes participant when he is aware of the priest-nun-priest sequence in the murders, and here again he is fed just enough to feel success without real revelation. The veteran, with his more highly developed awareness of the Voice of Cognition, senses something more esoteric, especially if he is familiar with the "pattern" stories that characterized the Golden Age detective novel.

This review of *The Rosary Murders* is, then, intended as an illustration of the transaction that takes place when the reader becomes involved (in this case, as privileged investigator) and the considerable degree of non-verbal meaning that is conveyed by process alone (the acts of focusing and interrupting, the signals and variations in pattern). It also suggests a method for interpreting the novel, designed for the formula story and more specifically for detective fiction.

What it offers is a theoretical base, a "handle" on the methodology of the detective story. Here is where Process Criticism has specific value. A reviewer can, for example, explain the structure of the novel and (by reference to the formulaic suspense structure) show how it fits into the traditions of its genre. Discussion of the handling of convention in a formula novel is a good approach to interpretation, especially if we take care to call attention to some of the variations that give this novel its identity. The reviewer should by all means point out devices handled with special skill, like focus and the other operational principles, the conditional plant, the fictional point of view, and the others we have been discussing in the preceding chapters. Process Criticism can, in addition, supply the basis on which to evaluate the book under review. Many reviewers appear hesitant to pass judgment on a novel, except to pronounce it a "good read" or to reject it with "I don't find this a good subject for a mystery." One of the best ways to assess the value of a book, of course, is to compare it with others of a similar kind, and analysis of process can supply a reviewer with a sound basis for such comparative judgments. We concluded Chapter 3 with some comments on the opening chapters of Robert Ludlum's *The Bourne Identity* as a textbook example of how to get a reader "hooked" and keep him that way. Ludlum's next book, *The Parsifal Mosaic*, was not nearly so successful as a suspense story, and a quick comparison of its first twenty-five pages with the same section of *Bourne* will show why. In contrast to the sharp drama of the conditional plant that opens *Bourne*, *Parsifal* begins with an array of four solitary figures that is soon reduced to two but then increased by five more. *Bourne* rivets the reader's attention on that one mysterious figure and the questions surrounding him, whereas *Parsifal*, long on solitary figures, is short on promissory plants. The weakness of the opening pages of *Parsifal* is finally betrayed by the early introduction of bare shock, when a big sex scene is interrupted by a K.G.B. man with a gun (22). To demonstrate the banality of all that, the interpreter need only recall the compelling promise left with the reader at the same point in *Bourne*, where the old doctor says, "With [the combination on the microfilm] you can open a vault in Zurich" (25). No amount of sensation or shock could rival the promise embedded in that plant.

We opened this discussion with some questions about the phenomenon of the Book You Just Can't Put Down. What makes it so, of course, is something that might be characterized as reader commitment. Rodell calls it "caring what happens next," and labels it, significantly, an art. To Daiches it is "an intensification of interest in what happens next," almost a paraphrase of Rodell's words except that Daiches's point of references is the reader, where Rodell's is the author. Both, as we have seen, are the concern of the process critic, who must take account of both as mediators between himself and the book he is seeking to interpret. The basic element, the reader, brings a variety of attributes to the act of commitment or, as Stowe puts it, the "transaction" with the text, including his own cultural shaping, which encompasses his previous experience with formula fiction. He is drawn into participation by the author's skill in supplying just enough knowledge, in hinting and suggesting (often by signals that have no meaning except as signals), and employing such strategies as focus, interruption, and intimation.

The task of the critic is to observe this process and to interpret it. To perform such a task successfully he must possess certain qualities, including an intense awareness of artistic purpose. He will unquestionably need a broad knowledge of fiction, especially in the genre he is interpreting. He must have an acute sensitivity to the presence of keys, patterns, and nuances in story-telling. Finally, and essentially, our process critic must be a venturesome spirit who does not shun innovative or creative approaches.

Notes

Chapter 1

[1]*Critical Approaches to Literature* (Englewood Cliffs NJ: Prentice-Hall, 1956), p.235.

[2]"Sherlock Holmes and Nero Wolfe: The Role of the 'Great Detective' in Intellectual History," in *Dimensions of Detective Fiction,* ed. Larry N. Landrum, Pat Browne, and Ray B. Browne (Bowling Green OH: The Popular Press, 1976), p. 89.

[3]*Mystery Fiction: Theory and Technique* (New York: Hermitage House 1952), p. 71.

[4]"Writing the Romantic Suspense Novel,"*The Writer,* 98, No. 6 (June 1985) 11.

[5]"Delay and the Hermeneutic Sentence," in *The Poetics of Murder,* ed. Glen W. Most and William W. Stowe (New York: Harcourt, 1983), p. 119.

[6]"Backward Construction and the Art of Suspense," in *Poetics of Murder,* p. 328.

[7]*Adventure, Mystery, and Romance* (Chicago: University of Chicago Press, 1976), p. 6. Subsequent references are included in the text.

[8]All three pieces are reprinted in Edmund Wilson, *A Literary Chronicle: 1920-1950* (Garden City NY: Doubleday, 1956).

[9]Timothy R. O'Neill, *The Individuated Hobbit* (Boston: Houghton Mifflin, 1979), p. 125. The Wilson review appeared in *The Nation* (April 14, 1956).

[10]*Detective and Mystery Fiction: An International Bibliography of Secondary Sources* (Madison IN: Brownstone Books, 1985).

[11]Editorial headnote, "Delay and the Hermeneutic Sentence," p.118.

Chapter 2

[1]Katherine Lever, *The Novel and the Reader* (New York: Appleton-Century-Crofts, n.d.), p. 43.

[2]*Art and Reality* (Garden City NY: Doubleday, 1958), p. 137.

[3]*The Craft of Fiction* (New York: Viking Press, 1957), p. 17.

[4]*Structuralist Poetics: Structuralism, Linguistics, and the Study of Literature* (Ithaca NY: Cornell University Press, 1975), p. 259.

[5]Cawelti, *Adventure, Mystery, and Romance,* pp. 6-7.

[6]Preface to *Celebrated Cases of Judge Dee* (New York: Dover, 1976), pp. ii-iv.

130   Suspense in The Formula Story

[7]This maxim has been variously stated by a number of writers. See Howard Haycraft, *Murder for Pleasure*, Revised Edition (New York: Bilbo and Tannen, 1974), p. 12.

[8]David N. Feldman, "Formalism and Popular Culture," *Journal of Popular Culture*, IX (Fall 1975), 394.

[9]*The Novel and the Reader*, p. 50.

[10]*Adventure, Mystery and Romance*, p. 17.

[11]"Narrative Structure in Fleming," in *Poetics of Murder*, pp. 113-14.

[12]"Delay and the Hermeneutic Sentence," p. 119.

[13]"Backward Construction and the Art of Suspense," pp. 331-2.

[14]Rosemary Herbert, "Murder by Decree: an Interview With John Mortimer," *The Armchair Detective*, 20 (Fall 1987), 346.

[15]*Art as Experience* (New York: Capricorn Books, 1958), p. 54.

[16]Walter Albert, "The Line-up," *The Mystery Fancier*, 4, No. 5 (Sept.-Oct. 1980), 9; Jiro Kimura, Letter, *The Armchair Detective*, 14 (Summer 1981), 247.

[17]Otto Penzler, "Crime Dossier," *Ellery Queen's Mystery Magazine*, November 1978, p. 41.

[18]*Critical Approaches to Literature*, p. 235.

[19]*Adventure, Mystery, and Romance*, pp. 17-18.

Chapter 3
[1]"The Concept of Formula in the Study of Popular Literature," in *Popular Culture and the Expanding Consciousness*, ed. Ray B. Browne (New York: John Wiley and Sons, 1973), p. 113.

[2]Cited by Ed McBain in *Eight Black Horses* (New York: Arbor House, 1985), p. 245.

[3]"Backward Construction and the Art of Suspense," p. 330.

[4] *Critical Approaches to Literature*, p. 235

[5]*The Technique of the Mystery Story* (Springfield MA: The Home Correspondence School, 1913), p. 40.

[6]*Aspects of the Novel* (New York: Harcourt, Brace, 1927), p. 87.

[7]"Suspense," in *The Mystery Writer's Handbook*, ed. Mystery Writers of America (Cincinnati OH: Writer's Digest, 1976), pp. 135-6.

[8]"Writing Action Fiction," *The Writer*, 86, No. 5 (May 1973) 12-13.

Chapter 4
[1]Rene Wellek and Austin Warren, *Theory of Literature* (New York: Harcourt, Brace, 1956), p. 129.

[2]Howard Haycraft, *Murder for Pleasure*, p. 12.

[3]"The Elements of Suspense," *The Writer*, 89, No. 2 (Feb. 1976) 16.

[4]*Adventure, Mystery, and Romance*, pp. 17-18.

[5]*Murder for Pleasure*, p. 38. Subsequent references are included in the text.

[6]Introduction to *The Omnibus of Crime* (New York: Payson and Clark, 1929), p. 46.

[7]*Mortal Consequences* (New York: Harper and Row, 1972), pp. 4-5.

[8]*Beyond Genre: New Directions in Literary Classification* (Ithica NY: Cornell University Press, 1972), pp. 6-7.

[9]W.H. Auden, "The Guilty Vicarage," in *Detective Fiction*, ed. Robin W. Winks (Englewood Cliffs NJ: Prentice-Hall, 1980), p. 18.

Chapter 5
[1]Howard Haycraft, *Murder for Pleasure*, p. 12.

[2]*Mortal Consequences*, p. 112.

[3]Jon Tuska, *Philo Vance: The Life and Times of S. S. Van Dine* (Bowling Green OH: The Popular Press, 1971), pp. 16-17.

[4]"Suspense and the Hermeneutic Sentence," p. 119.

[5]"The Art of the Detective Story," in *The Art of the Mystery Story*, New Edition, ed. Howard Haycraft (New York: Bilbo and Tannen, 1976), p. 11.

[6]"A Defense of Detective Stories," in *The Art of the Mystery Story*, p. 4.

Chapter 6
[1]In *The Mystery Writer's Art*, ed. Francis M. Nevins, Jr. (Bowling Green OH: The Popular Press, 1970), p. 102.

[2]"Dashiell Hammett," p. 200.

[3]*Beams Falling* (Bowling Green OH: The Popular Press, 1980), p. 19.

[4]"Poetics of the Private Eye," pp. 102-3.

[5]"Dashiell Hammett," p. 200.

[6] *Beams Falling*, p. 117.

Chapter 9
[1]Introduction to Hillary Waugh, *Last Seen Wearing...*, Mystery Library Edition (San Diego CA: University of California, San Diego 1978), pp. x-xi.

Chapter 10
[1]"The Spy," in *The Mystery Story*, ed. John Ball (San Diego CA: University of California, San Diego, 1976), p. 215.

Chapter 11
[1]"Delay and the Hermeneutic Sentence," p. 119.

[2]"Backward Construction and the Art of Suspense," pp. 328-9.

[3]*The Turn of the Screw* begins, "The story had held us, round the fire, sufficiently breathless..."

Chapter 13
[1]Sam L. Grogg, Jr., "Interview With Ross Macdonald," in *Dimensions of Detective Fiction*, pp. 185-6.

Chapter 14
[1]*Truth and Method* (New York: Seabury Press, 1975), pp. 345-9.

[2]"From Semiotics to Hermeneutics: Modes of Detection in Doyle and Chandler," in *Poetics of Murder*, p. 374.

[3] *Mystery and Its Fictions: From Oedipus to Agatha Christie* (Baltimore: The John Hopkins University Press, 1979), pp. 15-16.

Appendix

Editions of primary sources cited

Eric Ambler, *Journey Into Fear* (New York: Berkley, 1983)

Peter Benchley, *Jaws* (New York: Bantam, 1975)

William Peter Blatty, *The Exorcist* (New York: Harper and Row, 1971)

John Buchan, *The Thirty-Nine Steps* (San Diego CA: University of California, San Diego, 1978)

Raymond Chandler, *The Big Sleep* (New York: Ballantine, 1971)

Tom Clancy, *The Hunt for Red October* (New York: Berkley, 1985)

Len Deighton, *The Ipcress File* (New York: Fawcett, 1968)

Nelson De Mille, *Night of the Phoenix* (New York: Manor Books, 1975)

Daphne Du Maurier, *Rebecca* (New York: Literary Guild, 1938)

Ian Fleming, *You Only Live Twice* (New York: New American Library, 1964)

Frederick Forsyth, *The Day of the Jackal* (New York: Bantam, 1980)

John Gardner, *License Renewed* (New York: Berkley, 1982)

Michael Gilbert, *The Black Seraphim* (New York: Harper and Row, 1984)

Arthur Hailey, *Airport* (New York: Doubleday, 1968)

Dashiell Hammett, *The Maltese Falcon and The Thin Man* (New York: Vintage, 1964)

Jack Higgins, *Luciano's Luck* (New York: Dell, 1982)

Reginald Hill, *A Clubbable Woman,* Book Club Edition (Woodstock VT: Countryman Press, 1970)

William Kienzle, *The Rosary Murders,* Book Club Edition (Kansas City: Andrews and McMeel, 1979)

Fletcher Knebel, *Night of Camp David* (New York: Harper and Row, 1965)

Fletcher Knebel and Charles W. Bailey, *Seven Days in May* (New York: Harper and Row, 1962)

John le Carre, *The Spy Who Came In From the Cold* (New York: Dell, 1965)

Robert Ludlum, *The Bourne Identity,* Book Club Edition (New York: Marek, 1980)

Robert Ludlum, *The Parsifal Mosaic,* Book Club Edition (New York: Random House, 1982)

Ross Macdonald, *The Chill* (New York: Bantam, 1970)

Ed McBain, *Hail, Hail, the Gang's All Here!* (Garden City NY: Doubleday, 1971)

Lillian O'Donnell, *Casual Affairs,* Book Club Edition (New York; Putnam, 1985)

Lillian O'Donnell, *Ladykiller,* Book Club Edition (New York: Putnam, 1984)

Edgar Allan Poe, *The Selected Poetry and Prose of Edgar Allan Poe,* ed. T.O. Mabbott (New York: Modern Library, 1951)

Richard Martin Stern, *The Tower* (New York: Warner, 1974)

Peter Straub, *Ghost Story* (New York: Pocket Books, 1980).

Josephine Tey, *Three by Tey: Miss Pym Disposes, The Franchise Affair, Brat Farrar* (New York: Macmillan, 1954)

Janwillem van de Wetering, *The Butterfly Hunter* (Boston: Houghton Mifflin, 1982)

S.S. Van Dine, *The Greene Murder Case* (New York: Scribner, 1928)

Hillary Waugh, *Last Seen Wearing...*(San Diego CA: University of California, San Diego, 1978)

Cornell Woolrich, *Rear Window and Four Short Novels* (New York: Ballantine, 1984)

Index

135